Matters of Love

Published in the United States
by
Elevating Energy Press
elevatingenergy.com

ISBN-13: 978-0692770733
ISBN-10: 0692770739

First edition

Cover and book design by Grace E. Pedalino

Matters of Love

UNRAVELING
THE MYSTERIOUS ENERGY PATTERNS
OF
ATTRACTIONS AND RELATIONSHIPS

Dr. John Twomey

ELEVATING ENERGY PRESS

KNOW-FLOW-GROW

LIFE IS A MUSICAL SYMPHONY OF FEELING AND SOUND VIBRATING HARMONIOUSLY THROUGH OUR ENERGY FIELDS, TOUCHING OUR OWN UNIQUE PATTERNS OF ATTRACTION, EXPRESSION AND RELATING

The stars have not dealt me the worst they could do.
My pleasures are plenty, my troubles are two.
But oh, my two troubles they reave me of rest,
the brains in my head and the heart in my breast.

A.E. Housman

It is not what you say, but how you say it. *Sages of old*

There is no certainty. There only is adventure. *Assagioli*

The world is as you see it. *Sages of old*

We are all the same but different. *Sages of old*

Know yourself. *Socrates*

Intellectual knowledge is bondage. (*Jñanam bandha*)
Eastern proverb

Use your inborn creative potential.
Change from paper people to real people. *Fritz Perls*

To put it briefly, science can never threaten us.
Only persons can do that. *Carl Rogers*

Table of Contents

Note: Names and some features of individuals described in this book have been altered in order to maintain confidentiality.

WARNING: INDIVIDUALS WITH SERIOUS MENTAL HEALTH ISSUES ARE ADVISED TO DISCUSS THE FEASIBILITY OF THESE PRACTICES WITH THEIR PHYSICIAN OR THERAPIST.

To my wife Meredith who showed me what love is all about.

INTRODUCTION

There is always some madness in love, but there
is always some reason in madness.

NIETZSCHE

WHAT'S IT ALL ABOUT?

A re you aware that your neurons are generating energy
patterns that influence how you see the world and how
you express yourself in a relationship? When you read this book
you will learn why you are awestruck when you see a beautiful face
and find yourself longing for a happy state of enchantment, love
and connection. You will become aware of how your rationally
thinking mind is constantly attempting to find a reason for your
emotional brain driven love searching desires. You will begin
to understand your hungry heart's craving. You will decipher
the sometimes pleasant and sometimes unwelcome aspects of
the emotional outpouring and expletives that can spontaneously
and unexpectedly surge from deep within you.

This book is the result of five decades of counseling people
from all walks of life. I have treated combat veterans from many
wars as well as people simply seeking answers and solutions to
the needs, conflicts and anxieties of their everyday lives. I have
shared both the struggles that they have encountered while
searching for love and their joys in finding and maintaining
meaningful relationships. Over the years many of my students
have asked me if there was something that they could read about
the energy patterns that would surface during our interactions
with the patients we were treating. There has been nothing
written, however, that describes the pragmatic and collaborative

1

approach that I use to unravel the complexities created by an intense desire for love, connection and completion. I encourage my patients to explore these confusing, conflicting, and yet enticing, energy patterns being channeled from their emotional and reptilian brain structures as we explore their quest into matters of love. Why is it such a struggle for a person who really feels intense love for someone to express petty resentments to this person? What holds us back? Amazingly, when the painful, emotionally flooding trivial feeling is shared we make up. Love becomes stronger as the tension from this chaotic, dark energy field surfaces and releases. If you are searching for a relationship, you will gain some insight into why you can be initially attracted to somebody and later on down the road feel totally repulsed by the same person. Our minds reverberate with questions and challenges in our attempts to find the reasons why.

I share with you many of my patients' and students' intriguing stories of love. They are my teachers. Their own unique situations and solutions in these mysterious planes of love searching, and even love avoiding will have your hearts beating with excitement and wrenching with pain. I offer you insights and my techniques into how to let go of your painful experiences of the past and to move forward and live in the present.

First you will meet Frankie and Molly. The story of their unexpected meeting and healing relationship shows us the complicated excitement and pain of maintaining a loving and caring commitment. Corrine, June, Cameron and Claude are Iraqi war veterans. You will read about their heartbreaking struggles with war trauma and relationship complexities. I even share with you some of my own love searching adventures and the many professional training experiences that influenced my understanding of and perspective on love related issues and solutions.

As we proceed you will begin to see that we are often

struggling to express our deep emotional feelings and sensations. In fact, we are often only using metaphors, or sometimes even resort to cursing, to express ourselves in our relationships. Gradually you will become aware of how limited our rational brain functioning can be in matters of love. After all, Plato said love is a madness. I say love is also mysterious.

After reading this book you will be able to refine and rethink your own personal perspective on your unique matters of love. The needs, conflicts and anxieties that are getting in your way may begin to recede as you pursue your quest to find that emotional loving closeness and connection that your heart is yearning for.

BOOK ONE

1.

MY PATIENTS: MY HEROES

FRANKIE AND MOLLY:
RECOVERING FROM BATTLE, FINDING LOVE

Frankie's Story

Frankie still considered himself a golden child even though he was now in mid-life. He was conceived shortly after the end of World War II as a celebration of new life and joy. His dad had survived the trauma of intense battle and was grateful to be back home with his wife. Frankie was the first of twenty-two cousins to be born into this baby boomer generation. His childhood was idyllic as he nestled in the bosom of his big Irish family. With nine loving aunts, Frankie basked in a childhood of happy interactions and loving care.

"I was not one that was ever neglected," he recalled. Happiness, joy and celebration surrounded him in the myriad of festivities and functions found in a large loving family.

Flame-haired, Frankie was like a beacon on the sports field. Robust and strong from his mother's and aunts' good home cooking, Frankie developed an avid interest in baseball as he learned from his dad how to play shortstop. Even more importantly, he learned to bat on both sides of the plate. Switch-hitting was an art form that Mickey Mantle had demonstrated and all the young lads seriously interested in the game wanted to develop this skill.

"Never know what this might do for you in the future," Frankie's dad told him. When Frankie won the Little League batting title at the age of twelve, he had a whole family in his cheering section.

This golden child developed into a handsome youth as he played baseball, football and basketball. His entire family was so proud of him. He became the role model for all his younger cousins.

College time was approaching and Frankie chose to accept a navy officer's training scholarship. He excelled both academically and in sports. The entire clan celebrated his college graduation and commission in the U.S. Navy Reserve.

"There is only one thing that can happen to you now, young man, that is, go down," said his uncle Wally in jest. Frankie never forgot those words. They were like a melody playing in the back of his head.

It was only a matter of months before Frankie found himself in a new world, in the midst of the madness of the Vietnam War. The idyllic, loving years of his youth dimmed in the horror of the reality into which he had been thrust. He was first assigned to intelligence work and attending to senior officers. This gentle baptism into military life was short lived. Frankie had always loved adventure, but it took on new meaning as he began an intense naval assignment on an advanced tactical navy support base on the Mekong Delta. He was the replacement officer for a lieutenant who had been shot and killed.

The natives offered him fish heads and rice as a token of their hospitality. His stomach churned as he made the excuse that he had just eaten a peanut butter sandwich.

Frankie soon began to experience intense anxiety listening to the distant rumble of mortars and rockets echoing deep in the jungle where the worn down floating river docks serving as a base were situated. The heavy responsibility of making decisions about bombings and tactical maneuvers was inducing hypertension symptoms in this young officer. Holding his breath while the bombs were exploding was one of his coping tactics. Frankie's inner voice would speak to him.

"Did these bombs kill innocent women and children? How do I tell their loved ones about the death and injuries of my sailors who were wounded or killed in action? Can I say something that is honest and at the same time be comforting? Do I have enough information to make a proper decision as to which areas I should attack today? I feel responsible for everyone's actions. I am in charge. I am on my own. I get little help from the powers that be. They are in Saigon acting official, rational and proper during the day and partying, playing and drinking at night. I am a sucker for duty. This is not a sporting event with an end. I cannot go home when the game is over. It is with me every minute."

Sleepless nights brought on weariness, weakness and fatigue, as Frankie struggled with these issues. He had been trained by the Jesuits to trust his inner instincts. In the days leading up to a major attack on his base, he began to experience intense anxiety. Intelligence reports had identified a highly trained Vietnamese regiment that was heading in his direction. He had several radio consultations with intelligence personnel who assured him that there was no imminent danger, that the enemy was many miles away. Frankie's inner psychic states and energies felt different. His gut feeling signaled intense apprehension.

"Maybe I am too tired and jumpy," he berated himself. He chose to listen to the tactical reports that he was receiving from Saigon and did not order his base to be on a high state of alert. The sailors under his command did not seem to experience the apprehension that Frankie felt as they went about their routines. Their evenings were carefree as they relaxed, watched movies and drank beer. To make matters more confusing and anxiety-provoking, Frankie was informed that his Vietnamese interpreter had taken an unannounced leave. Doubt and suspicion further fueled his anxiety; this defection seeming to confirm his sense of imminent danger. Action was required. He radioed a request for more military assistance to deal with the impending attack. There was no reply for a long time. Then a brief response informed him that he was on his own and to do the best he could. Frankie became more agitated and restless. The doubts and anxieties of long-shadowed, sleepless nights became his companions in the darkness.

Without warning, a gigantic mortar round hit the base, slamming into the movie hall filled with relaxing off-duty sailors. Tracer rounds began to flash. Multiple .50 caliber mortar rounds were rapidly overtaking and destroying this floating-dock base. Frankie leaped to alert, giving instructions to his sailors and sending radio messages for help. In that moment a major crisis developed. Two men in ragged clothing, too far away to identify, emerged from a nearby jungle sub-base onto a thin-roped suspension bridge. They were attempting to enter the main base. The young navy guards were screaming at Frankie for orders to shoot. These guys were definitely armed and dangerous. Protocol would be to shoot them.

Frankie was dealing with the continuous stimuli of fire, shrapnel and mayhem, but his inner voice told him this was different. "Don't fire. Let them come," he shouted.

And so two American pilots who were commanding navy planes from a distant air base did not become part of the nightmare of carnage. They ran and jumped onto evacuating riverboats.

In the midst of this crisis and the many demands made upon him, Frankie realized that the goal of the mission had changed from defending the base to evacuation and avoiding capture. The Vietnamese had offered a huge reward for Frankie's capture because of his status as an intelligence officer. To be on the safe side, Frankie ripped off his officer's insignia and tried vainly one more time to send a message in the radio room.

Running next to the dock, he discovered that the pontoon boats had all raised anchor. Heavy fire rained everywhere. A severely wounded sailor lay on the dock writhing in pain. Frankie shouted in a loud, commanding voice for a boat to return. In that moment of pause he began to experience fear and panic. Would the sailors hear him? Would he be taken prisoner? Luck was with him as the coxswain turned one of the boats back to shore. Frankie tried to help the wounded sailor to his feet. His arm was dangling from his shoulder, severed from his body and hanging by a thread of bloody muscle. Sailors from the returning boat rushed to help Frankie drag the wounded sailor onto their boat.

Frankie often recalls the horror of this night. Buildings were burning; ammunition was exploding in the storage sheds. His men were dying. Rockets and tracer rounds were blasting overhead as Frankie was preparing to slide himself into the riverboat. Enemy troops were approaching the base on the rope bridge.

Suddenly, Frankie was hit by a round. He recalls turning his neck to the left as if he were standing at home plate with a ninety-five mile an hour fastball heading straight for his head. This automatic motor response from deep in his brain and psyche saved his head from being blown off. Thoughts of Uncle Wally's words of "going down" flashed through his mind, but this was different. Frankie was thrown into the air before he went down. He says that he was, "out for a bit," but not too long, because the boat was still in the mouth of the river. He found his vision was blurred and there was a sharp sting in his neck.

He lost consciousness and described returning to nightmare awareness as he slowly scanned his body. All of his fingers could fit inside a hole in his neck that was almost the size of his fist. The corpsman medic was attempting to bandage his wounds while Frankie tried to speak to him. He could form no words. His throat was gushing with blood. He was not totally conscious. In his dazed state he observed the wounded sailor propped into a sitting position heroically attempting with one arm to use the radio to get help for the crew.

Frankie told me his symptoms intensified. He began experiencing severe breathing difficulty. Blood was flowing copiously from his chest and mouth. He could not speak. All he could do was blink. He felt as though he was going to die any moment.

"I realized that I just couldn't get any air. I knew I couldn't keep breathing. The blood was choking and gagging me. Time was standing still. There was nowhere to go, nothing to be done."

With the assistance of two sailors, the corpsman moved Frankie and changed the position of his neck so that he could breathe more easily. Opening his air passage helped reduce the choking sensation, the horror of feeling the life force leaving his body.

Frankie was now a little more alert as he observed the entire shoreline ablaze, his base smothered in flame and smoke. It was all burning. Frankie felt horrible.

"It is all my fault," he thought to himself. "If I only listened to my own guts and instincts, this might not be happening."

Finally, the call for help was answered. Navy rescue planes flew overhead, assisting with air support for the escaping sailors. Just then, another young sailor corpsman came over to offer him comfort. He began cleaning Frankie up, holding his hand and offering words of comfort. Frankie recalls how sweet, loving and tender the healing touch of this young medic was. Relief surged through Frankie as helicopters arrived, lowering their metal baskets to rescue the wounded men and rush them to emergency treatment.

Neurosurgery was performed on Frankie with remarkable success. He was extremely fortunate that there was a highly skilled neurosurgeon at the hospital. His comment was, "We have no idea why you are alive. The miracle is between you and your God. There is not one physician here that understands why you are not a quadriplegic. You had enough shrapnel in you to fill a dump truck. The shrapnel missed your carotid artery by no more than the thickness of a butter knife. Don't thank me for what I did, my friend. Thank whomever you pray to."

Frankie spent the next month in the hospital recovering from his wounds. His hospital roommate was the young radioman who had had his arm nearly severed from his body. They began chatting, but were required by navy protocol officer and enlisted to be distant and respectful. Frankie nevertheless began to chat with the navy sailor, Ryan, looking for a topic to break the ice of reserve.

"Those tattoos look very impressive." Frankie spoke in a pleasant and friendly tone.

Ryan responded, "You haven't seen anything yet."

It was very hot and humid. He was lying on the bed covered only by a sheet. With a sudden flick he threw off his sheet. Frankie was amazed, stunned and titillated. Ryan was bedecked with tattoos all over his chest, stomach and even his groin.

Frankie says that he completely lost any capacity to say something meaningful or rational. He had descended into that world where there are no real words, but only a sensation of bewilderment. With a nod, Ryan continued his display by pointing to a tattoo on his penis.

"That's a bumble bee and when I get excited its wings spread out." Frankie took note of his own reaction. It was as if he stopped breathing, almost like the time when he was mortared. There were no thoughts, no words, just a sensation of awe. An event and image like this stay with someone for the rest of their life. This is one of Frankie's favorite stories.

The sailor pulled the sheet back up over himself and

warmed to the care and interest that Frankie showed toward him. He shared his fear that his wife would not want him back. The doctors had reattached his arm that had been almost totally blown off, but would never be completely normal. He asked Frankie to write his wife a letter and tell her about his injury, asking her to be merciful to him when he came home. Frankie did. He felt the pain, the anguish, the psychic wounds that this brave navy man was suffering following his injury.

Tears flowed from Frankie's eyes as he was telling me that he wrote to the sailor's wife and told her how much Ryan loved her and asked her to stand by him. He had met one of the most playful beings, and at the same time one of the most anguished persons, he had ever known. The bumblebee tattoo was an image that would be difficult to erase from his mind. All the different events of the monstrous attack and aftermath rattled in his mind for supremacy and release.

Frankie's return home was celebratory for his family, but not for him. His thoughts would drift back to the night his base was blown up. He would sink into the nightmare of the blinding lights and deafening roar of the mortars. He was feeling sad, sullen and remorseful in the deep recesses of his mind.

"I should not be here. I should be dead with all the others," he would think to himself. He was experiencing strong survivor's guilt. Being a part of the Irish culture, he acted as though he was happy and cheerful in the presence of his parents, aunts and cousins. Physical symptoms of rapid heartbeat, sweating and bodily tremors began to present themselves, easing their insidious path through Frankie's weak defenses. "I am still there mentally," he would think to himself.

During the summer months, Frankie returned to the comforting ocean community where he spent his high school and college days. He worked as a lifeguard and caretaker for the town. He began to socialize and reconnected with an old girlfriend. A few months of peace prevailed as he tried hard to put aside the nightmares still with him from the terror of the bombing of his base. At social gatherings he refused to drink alcohol with his many friends. He enjoyed sipping a few bottles of water while he engaged in light-hearted conversation. He found his mind became quiet when he ran, running for miles on the sandy beach at daybreak. Sleep was nearly impossible. He worked hard to restore his body to the once slender, athletic build he enjoyed as a youth. His scars were very obvious and would frequently generate questions about their origin. He had had plastic surgery on his face and neck with only moderate success. Vietnam was still mirrored on his body.

He was not uncomfortable telling people what had happened. Shame was a powerful feeling that he worked hard to overcome as restlessness and futility took hold of him. In our discussions Frankie was well aware of this paradox as he sought a philosophical explanation for these contradictory states of mind. Questions about the meaning of his life were his constant inner companions.

Over the next few years Frankie began many professional jobs. Each time he could not sustain the pressure and responsibility required by his duties. He finally decided that he would only work in the summer. He spent his time visiting and staying with his many cousins. He was still their hero, but someone whose rising star had taken a plunge, just as his Uncle Wally had prophesied.

This prelude is background information so that you know Frankie too. I want to share with you my twenty-five years of relating to, and treating him. He was a bright, energetic, and articulate person with a very playful side to his personality. All of these attributes for success were disrupted by his war experiences. He was constantly attempting to run away from these experiences. He displayed all the symptoms of post-traumatic stress disorder. These included nightmares, heavy heart pounding, sleep disturbance, and sensitivity to loud noises.

His major symptom was a strong survivor's guilt that he should not be here. He should have died like all the rest.

"If only I was more cautious and attentive, so many people would not have been killed," was his recurring lament during our dialogues. If Frankie stayed away from the stresses of everyday life, he could be OK. He reported that he had long restful days after our sessions, but then the horrific war remembrances would return.

Frankie had a special madness in his psyche. It would command and run his life. It would dictate his actions and reactions. His need was to create an anxiety-provoking situation that he could handle. He would humble himself by doing menial jobs in construction as a carpenter or laborer as a means of keeping busy. His friends provided professional jobs for Frankie that he would start, do well in for a month and then abruptly quit. These job stressors would bring on his symptoms of rapid heartbeat and cold sweats, along with racing thoughts. Inertia and depression would follow. He was a hound of heaven and sometimes hell.

In his romantic life, Frankie had reconnected with his college girlfriend, Patricia. He was able to express and share passionate intimacy with her. They had a mutual interest and enjoyment for boating and a love for the sea. They spent many warm summers together, but Frankie would withdraw in the fall and winter. For a while Patricia tolerated this pattern of interaction and withdrawal, but then began to realize that her biological clock was ticking. She pressed Frankie to make a commitment to her. He gave her a ring, hoping to make her happy. Another year went by and he would not commit. She returned his ring. He was crushed, anxious and relieved. He withdrew and became sad, angry and sullen, a grown man in his thirties without a mission. He was still reliving his trauma. It would not recede into the past, making it hard for him to have genuine warm and loving feelings on a consistent basis.

When Frankie discovered that the love of his life, Patricia, had taken up with a new love, madness, pain, sadness and rage took over Frankie's psyche. Tom, her new love, had been part of the beach crowd. Action was required. It was not in his personality constellation to respond in a passive way. Frankie was not someone who would just run away. He was consumed with a powerful energy that the ancient Greeks called *menos* that he felt in his chest. A wild, boiling rage began to possess him. Without thinking, he found himself breaking into Patricia's house. He watched his out-of-control self take a number of his belongings and a few of hers. The TV was the main item. When Patricia returned home she was aghast at what she discovered. Her place had been ransacked and violated. She called the police. Frankie was sought as the prime suspect.

Frankie arrived at my office in a state of panic. He was about to be arrested by the police for breaking and entering. He had returned to his hometown after his out-of-control rampage. His heart was pounding and his chest felt like it was about to explode. He could not sleep. He felt very foolish about his goings on. He was despondent and shamefully confessed that he felt like dying. The police had called his home and informed him that he was the prime suspect in the breaking and entering. "Your fingerprints were on the door. We know it was you."

As his therapist and healer, I knew he could not handle such a stressful confrontation. He was already flashing back to his base being bombed and burned. Individuals who relive these horrific events experience excitement and a maddening adrenaline rush in an attempt to release the overwhelming energy flooding their psyche. Just talking about and reviewing the break-in would not be enough for Frankie. His need to go over and over what happened (obsessive compulsive behavior) was beginning to surface. As he talked, he became more anxious and agitated. After an extensive period of listening and calming his mind, a creative problem solving solution began to emerge as we collaborated on a plan to extricate Frankie from this coil. I suggested that he should say to the police, "My fingerprints are on the toilet too. I lived there." We both started to laugh and this eased Frankie's anxiety so that his tension began to subside. This humorous approach helped him cope with the intense shame and guilt he was feeling and also activate his thinking self. Frankie agreed that he should not return to the beach area.

"I still have a problem," Frankie said. "How am I going to get myself out of this? I still have the stolen goods."

"What do you think you should do?" I said.

Frankie began to chuckle. The tension was released in a mischievous cackle as he proposed a plan to solve his problem. This devious turn of mind is often seen in individuals who try to undo a situation brought on by their uncontrollable emotional behavior. He would recruit his cousins, George and Robby, to create some suspicion in the police's mind so that they would let up on him. They would procure official delivery uniforms and a truck and return all the stolen goods to Patricia's house. They knew she would not be at home because she traveled during the work week and had lived with Tom since the break in. The items were cleaned of fingerprints, packaged, and dropped off at her door.

Frankie was relieved that all the stolen stuff was out of his hands. It had just been an act of madness on his part; he had no desire to own the things he had taken. Frankie's attorney informed the police that he was experiencing acute PTSD symptoms and would not be available to meet for questioning for some time.

Frankie's pain at losing Patricia as a lover continued to torture him. He had thrown the returned engagement ring under his car seat and could not find it. He thought that his auto mechanic took it. Anxiety and obsessing began to cloud his mind.

"Look with a flashlight," I told him.

He did. The ring was right where he had thrown it.

The madness induced by his rejection and reaction to it served as a respite from the terrors of Vietnam. Frankie's personality eventually returned to his humorous self. His panic, anxiety and obsessive behavior began to diminish. He had planned to move far away from the crime scene as a means of making a new life and getting away from the intensity of losing Patricia and the break-in. He telephoned the police on his drive to Florida and politely informed them that he was no longer living in the area. All the madness was like a bad dream that receded into meaninglessness as the intense, emotional flooding fueling the break-in dissipated.

A VILLAGE IN IRELAND (three years later)

Following his flight from the New England area, Frankie took off to many places. He traveled around the world searching for an inner psychic peace and understanding about what happened to him in Vietnam. His journey eventually settled into a rotation from winter seasons in the Florida Everglades, where he would be reminded of the jungles in Vietnam, to summers on a farm in southwestern Ireland where he had spent idyllic visits during his boyhood with his family and cousins. The farm was the home of his maternal ancestors, a joyous place where long, sun-filled summer days and magical moonlit nights induced joy, hope and tranquility and permitted only occasional intense emotional outbursts. It was here in this quaint seaport village where Frankie felt his roots. He made casual acquaintance with the townsfolk and eventually here met his future wife.

During one of the local village festivals usually named for a saint, Frankie found himself socializing in one of the pubs drinking bottled water while the other patrons were favoring more potent liquids. There were not only local folks present, but also a number of other Europeans participating in the festivities. They were drawn to the soothing sounds of the magical, mystic,

Irish Sea. Many had purchased property so they could experience life in a quaint, convivial village where the mountains provided a background of stillness so that one could imagine being in touch with the elusive sprites of Irish lore and ethereal Mother Nature.

The jovial chatter of the pub's clientele suddenly stalled into a shocked silence as a short, autocratic, middle-aged man started hollering, screaming and slapping a much younger, red-haired Celtic woman. It appeared that she had made some unflattering remark about his size that set him off. The villagers were well aware that she was his mistress and were familiar with his vituperative outbursts and ranting that I call a spaz. This occurred most often when he was in an intoxicated state.

The sound of Rudy's arrogant, abusive voice set off in Frankie the familiar symptoms of rapid heartbeat, sweating and intense anger that he had experienced the night when the mortars and rockets streamed over his base in Vietnam. To Frankie's, and everyone else's, surprise he suddenly found himself in the middle of the fracas. He had wedged himself between Rudy and the young woman, feeling the same compulsive drive to neutralize a perceived wrong as he had felt with Patricia. Echoing in his head was the haughty voice of the smug senior naval officer in Saigon who had wanted to report Frankie for being out of uniform after he had undergone surgery for his injury following the attack on his base. He began re-experiencing the rage he had felt toward this officer, but was well aware of his surroundings and with whom he was dealing.

"No man behaves this way in my presence," stated Frankie in an authoritative voice, his military bearing taking over.

"Mind your own business," replied Rudy in a haughty, condescending tone.

Frankie's brawny six-foot-three frame towered over the diminutive Rudy.

"I never back down from what I believe is right," was Frankie's response.

The frenzied look in Frankie's eyes terrorized Rudy. His complexion turned ashen, his madness tamed in the face of physical threat.

The entire village talked about this event for weeks.

Frankie and the young woman, Molly, experienced an immediate powerful connection. They were instant soul mates. There seemed to be a symbiosis of their heartbeats and souls. So, two people already turned forty, both veterans of many previous relationships all having gone sour for one reason or another, meet in the midst of the madness of a spaz in an Irish pub, sometimes referred to as a shrine because great madness and love can be experienced there. Out of this thunderous, energetic explosion emerged a couple who felt perfectly connected and totally in love.

Frankie whispered, "Let's get out of here." They walked out hand in hand, leaving Rudy shocked and bewildered. As they strolled under the moonlight back to his cottage the Irish fairies showered them with blessings and bestowed upon them a romantic potion. Two hounds of the earth had reconnected and reunited with the life force. Ten years of living and sharing was about to begin.

With the great love and tender caring that couples in midlife recognize and cherish, Frankie and Molly shared their backgrounds. We know Frankie's story. Molly's was just as intriguing. She, unlike Frankie, was not her parent's love child. Her father was a World War II pilot who flew numerous airstrikes into enemy territory. During one combat mission his plane was hit by enemy fire. His parachute got tangled in rough terrain. He thought he was about to die. Remarkably, he survived with minor injuries, eventually returning to combat with his squadron. After the war he worked as an aircraft engineer. His angry outbursts and alcohol abuse dominated Molly's childhood years. She was a victim of his moods and received many a thrashing. In her school years she excelled, receiving a doctorate in biochemistry. She taught college and at the same time conducted pioneering, controversial, psychopharmacology research.

Molly, like Frankie, had her own encounters with the law. She even spent some time in prison because she would not testify against her colleagues' illegal pharmaceutical research and activities. Exhaustion, depression, the loneliness from a failed romantic relationship and eventual incarceration dictated that she take a respite from her college teaching and research pursuits. Soon thereafter she met Rudy. At first he was very loving to her, but within a few years he was mistreating her in many ways. The love was still there, but it was mad. It is no wonder that she became Rudy's victim.

Molly had yearned to reestablish her professional life, but had been unable to extricate herself from Rudy's control. Frankie did that for her and offered much more in terms of caring for her and understanding her difficulties. Molly loved to sail, bike, and swim, the same activities Frankie enjoyed. She was seeking to contact her real, authentic, self. Her troubled inner psychic core had been manifesting intense anxiety and agitation, much in the same way that Frankie's war experiences would flood his mind and impair his capacity to function.

A strong attachment and caring began to evolve between Molly and Frankie as they shared each other's pain in the context of the joy of their love. Rudy, meanwhile, sent emissaries and even threatened to kill Frankie if he did not return Molly. Rudy wanted his "property," but Frankie stood his ground and informed them that Molly chose to be with him. Molly was glowing as she felt so protected and emotionally connected to her new love. She had met, and now cherished, someone with whom she could relate and share her past, her troubles and her goals.

In a quaint, cozy, teashop in Ireland's capital city of Dublin,

Frankie proposed marriage to Molly. He gave her the pet name Molly, for the renowned Molly Malone, a pretty fishmonger who roamed the streets of Dublin singing and selling her wares.

They married within the year and returned to the U.S. Frankie was proud to present Molly to his family. She was welcomed by some and shunned by others. In the dynamics of family relationships sometimes a family member's significant other is considered not good enough. Fortunately, most were happy to meet the gregarious, but humble, couple. Frankie brought his bride to make my acquaintance and to request individual and couple's therapy. Our first of many sessions began.

Frankie and Molly experienced all the emotions of love with its myriad intricacies, intimacies and knotty issues. Frankie's emotional symptoms of hypertension, anxiety, panic and restlessness began to diminish in intensity as he shared with Molly the many events of his military traumas. As a highly verbal, intelligent woman, she was able to organize and sequence his tales of war. She took notes and would present them to him for dialogue and discussion. They composed a manuscript about these events. This process generated both excitement and healing. While this literary work was in progress they also engaged in vehement psychic battles as they argued over what and how to say it.

All good lovers develop this playful, surrendering, nonjudgmental trust, to share their inner psychic thoughts and feelings. Frankie's and Molly's entire psychic expressions of love, sadness and intense emotional outbursts, that I would term spazzing, were a part of this process. Molly would frequently express her rage and anger at Frankie. She had been physically beaten in her earlier life and previous relationships. She made a present of that to him. She could sit for hours by herself practicing the three "S's," sitting, sucking and sulking. Her dark night of the soul manifested itself in a different manner than

Frankie's.

It is my contention that a couple is not really in a long-term relationship unless these spazzing, intense, emotional expressions, are allowed to surge and release the tension. This is not about physical violence, but rather acknowledging the reactions and resentments that rise up in relationships. Listening to, and not judging our lover's experiences and complaints are major components of a successful relationship. Resentments are often misdirected at the person one loves, when their source is most frequently another person or former lover. In my clinical experience, I have observed that men tend to spaz earlier in the relationship and then settle in and merge with their beloved. Women often attend initially to developing and enriching the relationship and wait until later to allow their resentments voice. The content of the intense emotional reaction and madness is most often secondary to a previous event that is activating the limbic brain reaction (the spaz). It initially surges like an erupting thunderstorm, runs its course and flows away softly and silently, if not interfered with intellectually. Love has its own methods for releasing tensions and drawing us closer to the ones we love. The *South Pacific* lyric, "Fools give you reasons, wise men never try," is true in situations like this.

This was the case with Molly and Frankie. Initially, Molly listened to Frankie's horrific war experiences and even helped him write about them. As she became more comfortable, Molly expressed her resentments to Frankie. A gentle, peaceful, state would follow these intense emotional expressions because Frankie allowed them to flow without interference or recrimination, as Molly did with Frankie. Learning to listen and be the target for the intense emotional expression, which I call taking the hit, generates more love and connectedness than verbally arguing who is right. Love is not an intellectual issue, it is the manifestation of a surging, psychic energy that cannot be captured in a truly rational sense. I am not talking about physical abuse, but rather, of allowing pent up emotional states to be released without challenge in order for growth and creativity in the relationship to emerge and make the couple a happy, wholesome, thriving unit. If this misdirected tension and anger, often a result of previous relationships, is defused, then the heartbeats of the couple unite into the oneness of their love.

Molly and Frankie spent many blissful rewarding years in the United States, primarily in coastal Florida. They healed each other in their own inner psychic way. About six years into the marriage, Molly developed breast cancer. She began a series of medical treatments that reawakened much of her early inner psychic pain. Frankie tried his hardest to be supportive as Molly's dark side emerged. She often would not speak to him for days. He attempted all of his humorous Irish techniques to lighten her load. He ran a local road race with a slogan written on his T-shirt: "Save Second Base. Fight Breast Cancer."

Intense soul-searching and yearning became the lifestyle for Molly. She felt she was not "at home" in the U.S. She longed to be back in her native land and to reconnect with the sweet, serene sensations and experiences of her youth. Frankie was at a loss for words. For him, cold European winters were too difficult to take. Nevertheless, they did return to the village in southwest Ireland where they had met. They arrived to a dark, dreary, lightless December. Their energy began to deplete. Exhaustion set in. Frankie felt low. The dark night of the soul, the emptiness, nothingness and despair that he had read about in his Jesuit college theology classes began to overtake his cheerful outer self. Depression set in. Molly needed more medical treatment. They both agreed to return to the U.S. where Molly had already received treatment. When they arrived, Frankie's cousin, Owen, offered them his mountain cabin for a restful two weeks. Here they felt nourished and rejuvenated.

The following week we had a very emotional session in my office. Their companionate love was fading and altering as

Molly was physically failing. Both she and Frankie lived with the daily anxiety that her physical existence was coming to an end. She spazzed at Frankie every day and blamed him for ruining her life and not allowing her to grow in the manner that she wanted. Frankie held his ground and was well aware, with my assistance, that she was really emotionally reacting and reliving her earlier life experiences. He became the target for helping her to release the tensions from her multiple traumas and disappointments. He took comfort from knowing that she was close to a group of women in the community who knew nothing about her real background, but provided warmth and support by sharing mutual interests in poetry, philosophy and music. This helped her to endure the intense inner conflicts that were raging in her psyche.

He still felt the love and caring emanating from this wonderful woman as she was facing the imminence of death, but the numbness that he had so often experienced in his life was returning as he felt her slowly receding from him. Shedding a tear was something that was difficult for him to do. As an ex-warrior he took his "hits," but now he too began to develop serious medical symptoms, primarily heart related, that needed care and attention.

After much contemplation and dialogue, Molly decided to fly back to her homeland. She returned to Ireland to be with her brother and sister and the friends of her childhood. Eventually, she took up residence in a comfortable country cottage. There she wrote poetry, meditated and contemplated her approaching end of life issues. There was a bitter sweetness in parting from Frankie. The genuine love they felt when they met was slowly returning to their consciousness and igniting a tender awareness of each other. There was a gratitude for the love they had created together. The intense emotional rages and spazzing no longer surfaced, had run their course and dissipated like a raging waterfall that surges until it slowly runs out of moisture and dries up. Frankie had not fanned the flames of Molly's intense emotional expressions, so they were able to rekindle the embers of their love. Now there was just a psychic meeting of beings dwelling in physical bodies that surrendered their love to each other and the Life Force. Daily transatlantic phone calls and e-mails hummed with their vibrating psychic connection. They each recognized the other's journey of healing.

Late summer evenings had their own mystery and magic as Molly passed peacefully in her cottage. She had spent many months living life beyond the expectations of her medical providers. Light gardening, writing poetry and listening to music had healed her psychic wounds. Her time had come. Frankie exhaled. Ten years of love, joy, healing and commitment completed its cycle.

Frankie is back on his own now, more humbled, reflective and serene. His memory of Molly can still wrap him in the stillness and peace of the life force. As he walks the beaches, her thoughts, words, and inspiration live in his psyche as he works to separate himself from the madness of the night in Vietnam so many years ago.

2.

LOVE, BEAUTY AND TRAUMA FROM THE WAR IN IRAQ

Stories of love intrigue us. We have all had experiences of this mysterious love searching sickness and its accompanying compulsive behavior. We all try in varying ways, with varying amounts of success, to control these intensely surging energetic patterns. This love-driven, fiery, expressive energy demands recognition in defiance of our thinking and decision-making self.

MY BEST FRIEND'S GIRL: CAMERON, JERRY AND LOIS

In a triangular love situation things are even more complicated for everyone and always painful for at least one person. My patient, Cameron, tearfully related to me that he and his life-long chum, Jerry, had a major falling out over a girl. Cameron and Jerry had met as youngsters, played sports, been in scouts and gone to school together. In fact, they had done everything together and bonded as best buddies. In the next chapter I will describe my personal navy experiences on how young lads bond in a special psychic manner. They will do anything for each other until there is a woman involved.

Jerry started dating Lois during their junior year in high school. Cameron would join them for social activities from time to time. All was going well until the start of their senior year. Cameron became a little more successful athletically than Jerry. Lois became enamored of him and he responded to her invitation to date. Intensely romantic physical expressions of love followed. A boyhood friendship turned into mortal rage and animosity. What was once a loving closeness turned into scorn, disdain and bitterness. That ancient, Greek god-induced, energetic madness, *ate*, was running Cameron's life.

"This madness overtook me. We had one hell of a good time. There was nothing to say to Jerry. I felt bad for him, but my sexual organ was doing all the talking."

Jerry eventually persuaded Lois to go to a school outing with him and talk things out. Cameron did not seem to mind. He really did mind, however, when he received a phone call that evening and was told that Jerry and Lois were killed when Jerry ran his car into a tree.

Cameron was crushed. He had lost the two loves of his life. He became extremely quiet, withdrawn and depressed. He quit the football team and stopped attending school. He was inconsolable. His mom tried everything to help him. His dad was at a loss as to what to do. Everyone reached out to Cameron, but no one could provide comfort. After several months of just hanging around the house enveloped in inertia and nothingness, Cameron enrolled in an alternative high school and completed the requirements for his diploma. He worked off his tension by getting a part-time job cutting down trees. This required hard labor that tired out his body. It helped to diminish the anxiety and guilt torturing his emotionally flooded, anguished mind.

The war in Iraq was underway and Cameron decided to join the Marines Corps. Eventually, he was deployed to Iraq. His fantasy was that he would get maimed and destroyed in an explosion as punishment for his evil deed. To his surprise, his depression lifted. He became an outstanding marine and was rapidly promoted to sergeant. He led combat missions and was involved in many intense firefights, and was wounded in several battles. After a year of intense combat he completed his tour of duty and was discharged. That inner psychic feeling of loneliness, despair and guilt began to resurface when he returned to his hometown. He had hoped it had gone away forever as it had when he was in Iraq. Dreams of Jerry and Lois occupied his sleep nearly every night.

"Having a few drinks helps cuts down the pain," he shared.

"Can you find a new love?" I asked.

"It's too hard right now. I visit their graves every other day. I am part of them, but I am the only one here."

How can we help Cameron to begin to make a new life? His love for Lois and Jerry still dominates his heart and mind. The shame of his betrayal is foremost in his thoughts. The ancient physician, Galen, prescribed a distraction to alleviate the intensity of grief for a lost love relationship. This distraction provides a respite from the emotional intensity of the loss. Cameron's distraction was the war in Iraq. Unfortunately, his heart-aching loss resurfaced when he returned home and still continues. On several occasions he began therapy, but after a few sessions would quit.

"The intense pain is too much to take. I am tired of talking about it. That won't help the hole I feel."

We all hope that this decorated young veteran will be able to find a new love and recover.

CLAUDE:

Claude's story illustrates Love's powerful joy and sorrow in the healing process. He was in heavy combat and seriously injured in the intense fighting during the Iraq campaign. He served as a sergeant with the army, but had also been a navy medic before the war.

Claude grew up in a very strict household. He was his mom's love child. Like my patient Frankie, he loved baseball, but was not quite as skillful a player. Running track was his favorite sport for letting off steam. Following high school graduation Claude could not wait to escape the constrictions of his family's rules, especially in regard to sexual expression and romantic pursuits. So he joined the navy. He loved military life, but had a penchant, as young medics sometimes do, for chasing women, drinking beer and being somewhat obnoxious. His behavior did not sit well with his superiors and after extensive counseling and multiple attempts to change his lifestyle, he was not allowed to reenlist. Totally shocked by this rejection, Claude came home, quit drinking and started attending junior college classes. One of his goals was to become a physician.

Claude applied himself and did well in school, but the lure of the military lifestyle still held a strong attraction for him. Caught up in the furor of 9/11, he joined the army so that he could be an active combatant. To maintain sobriety was his objective and to serve honorably was his driving passion. He rapidly advanced through the ranks and found himself in Fallujah camped in a tent and in charge of a unit.

Suddenly in Iraq, Claude was enmeshed in the same horror that Frankie had endured in Vietnam. He and his seventeen men were awakened by an intense mortar round that slammed into the area, wreaking havoc and horrendous destruction. Claude was knocked out by the explosion. When he first regained consciousness he was so disoriented he did not know what was happening. After several minutes he became groggily aware of his surroundings. As he looked around he could find only one other soldier at least partially functional. All the other men were seriously injured or dead. His old navy medic training took over as he did his best to provide first aid for as many of his men as he could. He felt moist droplets flowing from his head and ears. He was so busy in his rescue effort that he ignored the thin streams of blood dripping from his own body until a rescue medic arrived on the scene. As the medic bandaged his bleeding head, ear and leg wounds, Claude was in a daze. He remained stunned and confusedly tried to figure out what was going on.

Suddenly, Claude thought of his best buddy, Kent. They had spent the past year together, inseparable, trusting and very emotionally connected. Fear, terror and panic set in. As he recalled for me his experience, Claude described his frantic, berserk behavior while his memory was returning. He was moving about in a fog-like, frenzied search for Kent. Abruptly, time stopped. It was as if his life as he knew it had ceased for a moment. Kent was before him on the ground bleeding and unconscious.

"Why did I not look for him first?"

He felt totally devastated, wiped out, breathless and lost for words. Kent was going to die.

"My life is over," he began thinking to himself. Claude was inconsolable.

This story of losing their best buddy in battle is one that I have listened to over and over again from soldiers and marines. Men in combat situations often bond with someone with whom they experience a strong psychic connection, closeness and a feeling that is beyond words. It defies any satisfactory rational explanation. In my opinion, it is best described by Homer and Plato as a psychic manifestation of the madness of love. Kent would die in the next week. Claude was eventually shipped back to the U.S., feeling anxious and confused from the mortar blast that had knocked him out. He was treated in a U.S. military hospital for his injuries. Eventually, he returned to his hometown and obtained a job in the fire department. He became an outstanding paramedic and started to resume his studies to become a doctor, but the intrusive memories of the blast and the agony of losing his best friend hounded him every day. At night he contended with nightmares of the mortar rounds and during the day found himself snappy and shying away from people. He could be found at the local bar each evening drinking and feeling sorry for what had happened to him.

Hal, a chum from his grammar school days, tried to get him to go out and socialize. Claude consistently refused, but under pressure of Hal's relentless badgering he finally agreed to go to a strip club one Friday evening. The alluring eyes and enticing dancing of a dark-haired lady named Maria caught his attention. He felt a magical attraction to her that shocked him.

"It had the same intensity as the mortar attack," he whispered. Claude's energy and awareness became channeled into his heart center. A flame lit within him, enveloping his senses and directing all his energies toward Maria. Maria showed her approval of Claude's admiration. This exotic goddess was about to change his life. All the joy and divine madness of carnal love was ready to bloom.

Claude left Hal to fend for himself and spent the night with Maria. Soon they began living together, along with Maria's three-year-old daughter. Within a few weeks, however, Maria began physically beating up Claude. She smashed his arm with her wooden hairbrush that shattered from the force of her blow. He put up with it. The love, excitement and madness were consuming him. He even forgot Kent and what had happened in Iraq. He was now operating on a different level. Maria became his sole focus and he was obsessed with pleasing her. Their volatile verbal and physical exchanges reached well beyond their living space. The neighbors could not tolerate all the havoc, however, and soon the police became involved. Claude's friends even tried to persuade him that he was an asshole and jerk. They tried to convince him that this crazy love surge was total insanity and nothing positive would come of this out-of-control relationship. Eventually, the Department of Youth Services became involved because of the young child. She was soon taken from her mother. Maria was devastated. Speaking to the authorities, Maria laid the blame on Claude and told them that he was a batterer. This was believable since a vet is sometimes violent when he returns home from the war zone.

A restraining order was issued against Claude and he moved back to his own apartment. He and Maria separated for four months. Claude went back to school, but was still obsessed with his love for Maria. It was so difficult to stay away from each other that Maria would stealthily come to Claude's so that they could play their sexual game with all its excitement and physical violence.

Claude actually did not mind getting whacked. The sound and intensity of the beatings were reminiscent of the mortar blast he had experienced in the tent in Iraq. Needing to keep the rest of the world unaware of their secret meetings, however, the couple now imposed a new restraint on their sexual activity, tempering their breathing, yelling, and abuse. In place of their previous wild, surging expressions of the madness of their love, Claude and Maria yelled and beat and loved in a hushed, subdued quiet that actually intensified their bonding.

This relationship was fraught with difficulty, but the most challenging problem for Claude to deal with was that Maria was a chronic liar. She would twist a situation so that she appeared to be the victim.

"What am I going to do with you? You are such a liar," Claude would confront Maria.

"I want my baby back," she would respond.

These realities intruded into the confrontational madness of their intensely physical sexual activity, spurring Maria and Claude to adopt a more reflective perspective to express their commitment to each other and build a trusting, caring, relationship.

Claude had also developed a strong attachment to Maria's young daughter, but was not allowed to visit Maria after the child was returned to her mother. They moved to another city with separate apartments all supported by Claude. Couple's counseling provided support and caring, so that slowly Claude was able to persuade Maria to confess to the authorities that she was the instigator of the excessive physical behavior and that she was in fact beating him up. They would hear nothing of this. They decided that it was just a ruse on the couple's part to be allowed to live together. Eventually, an agreement was made that Claude had to undergo a 300-hour batterer's class and Maria had to attend a class for battered women. They were not allowed to live together during this time.

Claude dreamed of having a life and family with Maria. His friends told him he was a jerk and crazy and nothing good would come of this. He did not agree.

"We are going to get a life together. I still do miss Kent, but not as much. I feel guilty that I do not think of him like I used to. What do you think?"

"If things work out for you and Maria perhaps you could name one of your children for Kent," I answered.

Claude smiled,

"Thanks. You have given me hope. I am going to go to school and be a doctor. Maria is already in school. She has given up stripping. She wants a life. I want a life."

Claude's romantic involvement with Maria had energized him and was releasing the dark side negative tension generated by his combat experiences. Optimism for the future resurfaced and was restored though his interest in Maria.

CORRINE

Corrine's story of love and romance is also related to her life in the military. Being a soldier in an organization provided her with the self-esteem and support that gave her a reason for living. The army is her family. She had already served two tours in Iraq and was preparing for a third one. Corrine raised herself without a family. She never knew her father. Her mom had many sexual forays and had no use for her. She became a ward of the state and was placed in foster care. She was constantly harassed and preyed upon by adult friends of her caretakers. She told me that she spent many nights sleeping in the park or at her friends' houses. She was a good student and loved math. She had worked part time to support herself and managed to complete high school. Cheerleading and running track helped her to develop her self-esteem.

"I was one tough gal," she confided to me, "I knew how to get what I wanted and keep myself going."

Boyfriends were many. She did not want to commit to any serious relationships. Not until she joined the army did Corrine feel enveloped by a safe environment and structure that offered her comfort and a hope for the future.

This attractive young lady in her early twenties had been promoted to sergeant and recognized for her accomplishments. What bothered Corrine about her experiences in Iraq was not the many mortar and rocket attacks to which she was subjected, but the constant harassment that she had to put up with from senior soldiers who wanted to be sexually intimate with her. She even had to get a transfer from her first unit to another because her boss was making demands on her.

"We women had to deal with this all during our tour. We went on convoys together so we would not have to put up with these constant come-ons."

Corinne told me many stories about situations where people had been either killed or wounded. It was wrenching to observe children lying injured by the roadside. She felt helpless that she could not do something for them, but orders were to accomplish her mission. It was not even safe to help; some situations were set ups. Sleepless nights, rapid heartbeat and restlessness were chronic symptoms she had to endure. When she returned home to her civilian job Corrine could not work every day because she felt so depressed and restless and had difficulty focusing on her tasks. Her managerial team was very understanding of her situation and did not put pressure on her.

In her private social life guys would want to constantly attend to her by fixing her car and taking her to dinner. They would go out of their way to find a reason to be in her presence. Corinne viewed herself as a goddess who liked to engage with men, but only on her terms. After living with a local lad for six weeks, Corrine married him. She and Dusty spent the summer together before she began her second tour in Iraq. Then it was over. She met Will. She instantly liked him. They worked in the same unit in Iraq and after returning to the U.S., continued seeing each other.

"I thought I had problems, but his are worse. He hollers, screams and even punches me when we are sleeping together. I laugh and tell him to get help. He just smiles and says 'I have you.' I only see him once a week. That is enough."

Dusty, Corrine's legal husband, wanted to remain married even though he knew all about Will.

"He still loves me. I have affection for him. He had his turn. There is something nice and sweet about him, but that is it," she told me.

"It is hard for you to trust anyone, especially if they like you," I said.

"Ya, I feel this nauseous, restless agitation when someone is real close to me. My stomach knots. It's a sick feeling. I have to keep some distance," she says.

I sensed her heart was beating rapidly and her face was altering from a happy smile to a sad, empty look.

"What do you do to relax?" I asked.

"I like to run and go to the gym," Corrine replied.

She was tearful and very emotionally tense throughout our meeting. She told me during my psychodiagnostic evaluation for another deployment to Iraq, that she was not interested in counseling at this time.

"I had enough of this when I was young. I am on my own. I have to live with me. I know what it does and doesn't do. I know myself and what is really happening out there."

I then taught her the circle breath exercise that I will describe for you in chapter thirteen. Corrine thanked me for teaching her this technique and agreed to use it as one of her many tools for self-healing and improvement.

"Thank you for coming," I replied.

As we shook hands and I walked this resilient young woman to the waiting room I felt moved by her life story. Corrine ran her own show. Her psychological awareness was highly sophisticated. I could feel my heart reaching out to help her release her lifelong sadness during the circle exercise. Her strong, energetic healing resources and hope for a successful life and future were inspiring.

JUNE

June grew up in a suburb of a large city. Her parents, grandparents, aunts and uncles, showered her with love and admiration. She played softball and went out for track in high school. She had many friends. Her charm and beauty did not go unrecognized; she was elected captain of the football cheerleaders. June was a good student. Her career goal was to become a nurse. Her boyfriend, Nathaniel, was very clinging and wanted her to declare a firm commitment. He made no secret of the mad love and possessiveness he felt for her. June was not ready to commit, however, and wanted to get away, far away, from his intensity and clinging neediness. After much reflection and discussion with her guidance counselor she decided it would be best to postpone college for a few years. With the promise of many benefits, including her college education, June chose to enlist in the military.

After intense training as a medic she found herself stationed at a large trauma center in Iraq. She spent the twelve to fourteen hour workdays treating and caring for the continuous onslaught of seriously wounded marines and soldiers. These were not simple wounds, but injuries and trauma requiring intensive care. Slowly, exhaustion began to seep in as June struggled to offer all the care and comfort she could. She got little sleep.

Completely involved in her intense care for these heroes, June developed a great sensitivity to the emotionally love-starved needs of these young soldiers and marines. So many of them would cry out her name and ask her to hold their hand as they were dying. She would take a marine or soldier's hand in hers and brokenheartedly watch the last breath leave his body. June told me that there were hundreds of marines and soldiers hollering and begging her to attend to them.

When the time was up for her tour of duty, a new unit from the U.S. was assigned to her makeshift hospital. According to June, they did not know how to provide the necessary critical care for these trauma victims and as a result people died who could have been saved. She left Iraq angry, confused, agitated, and sleepless. Nightmares echoing with the voices of dying soldiers and marines crept into her few hours of rest. Those same voices could engulf her during regular waking hours; she called these times *daymares*.

I met June in my office. Her mom sat in the waiting room. June's sadness and dejection were plain to see on her worn and weary, but still beautiful face. Since her return, June had been snappy, argumentative and mean to the mother whom she had always loved dearly. Mom seemed to understand and tolerate June's vituperative outbursts. Her siblings were not as kind. They would tell her to get over it.

June no longer wanted to be a nurse. She was not sure what she wanted to do for a future career. She did not want to spend time or relate in any meaningful way with Nathaniel, her admiring, devoted boyfriend who was still very much in love with her. She just wanted to be left alone and be by herself.

June was a good athlete and loved the sea. She thought she would like to spend the summer working at her old high school job as a lifeguard. She was also coping with her trauma by running long distances. Yoga classes also helped her to release this intense stress. I suggested that medication would help improve her sleep. A treatment plan was initiated and counseling was arranged.

June displayed the emotional exhaustion of a comforting

and dedicated angel whose wings had been plucked by so much sorrow and death as she held in her loving arms so many dying warriors who left the world too early. Her role in the war that demanded her love and selfless attention, as well as her nursing skills, left her with a heart-wrenching residual pain that hid in the depth of her eyes and echoed in her voice for all to feel.

Counseling, medication for sleep, regular and non-talking therapies, such as yoga and aerobics, could help calm her body and mind. The surging psychic invasion she encountered will eventually begin to recede, but never go away. If she has a child, it will help heal her. I have observed this in many of my World War II and Vietnam patients.

BOOK TWO

3.

MY INTRODUCTION TO MATTERS OF LOVE

NAVY DAYS: THE 1960s

My Navy Adventures

As young, curious, thrill-seeking navy medics with lots of energy, my chums and I were intrigued by the romances that so many of us were encountering. What was behind the excitability and madness that we constantly created for ourselves? Why were we so enmeshed in all this drama? Intense sexual arousal has its own life. Biological explanations could offer some solace to the rational, thinking brain, but the excitability and madness would often win out. The F-word was constantly being expressed about almost everything, bombing my ears, shaking through my whole body and invading my rational thinking self's way of looking at things. What did my closest navy friends mean when they affectionately called me a *fucker?* What was all this chatter rattling my mind doing, forcing me to take note of what was happening in me and in everyone around me? Why were many of my fellow sailors often jumping from one partner to another, paying little attention as to how or why their relationships could or could not work?

During my college days I developed an intense curiosity about the biological components of sexual energy and its multiple methods of expression. My passionately-driven, anatomical safaris took me to discovering the function of a group of muscles that churn under our butt and flow beneath our body core pelvic floor area. This area is called the perineum. Its muscles are a major control center in mastering the biological functioning for our urinary and sexual activity. The ancient classical mystics were aware of this mysterious pulsating center and referred to this branch bundle of nerves as the seat of wisdom. The Far Eastern psychic science practitioners call this circulating, creative energy center flowing beneath the base of the spine *kundalini*. It is neither a good nor bad, somewhat subtle, love surging energy field, that is continually manifesting and expressing itself in its search for beauty and completion.

The major biological component of this process is related to our hormones and base brain. Many of my navy buddies' frequent, highly exciting sexual forays spurred my playful, metaphor-making mind to label this incessant love-seeking behavior as a disease called *kundalitis*. This can simply be stated as our old brute brain's manifestation of a continuous, intense pulsating sexual expressive energy that demands recognition and expression of its biological needs. This flowing energy pattern functions in a manner similar to the scientific principles of the recirculating nitrogen and oxygen cycles that simply state energy recirculates and cannot be created or destroyed.

FROLICKING FREDDIE

This term *kundalitis* was actually born after one of our close chums, nicknamed "Frolicking Freddie," became so excited and aroused when he met a navy medic, Suzie, that within days he proposed marriage to her. She appeared to be very warm, attractive, sensitive and caring. They wanted to make their vows of eternal devotion and commitment to each other in a candlelit ceremony and planned to have their wedding in just a few weeks. All their friends were invited. There was much excitement throughout the naval hospital compound. A huge hotel celebration was planned. As intuitive as I am in matters of love, I felt he was love sick and would later regret his actions. My advice was to have a celebratory engagement party instead. Freddie paid no ear to me. I refused his invitation to be the best man.

Minutes before the ceremony was to begin, Suzie disappeared. One of the guests went missing. Soon another guest was gone. It seems that a number of the young men who were invited guests visited the lovely bride all dressed in white before the ceremony. Freddie was heartbroken. Everyone had a great time but him. To be married was Freddie's goal. To be worshiped, loved, and adored was Suzie's goal. Freddie was seeking a lifetime of commitment. Suzie's rational, thinking mind deceived her into planning this commitment too, but her archaic brain's carnal, expressive hormones had an agenda of their own to biologically relate to as many men as would love her. Her primitive, expressive behavior pattern dominated and won.

Freddie's penance for his rush into a committed state of matrimonial bliss was that he was forced to hear the story of what had happened over and over again. He developed an excellent ability to tolerate that *Ha Ha* laugh of his so-called navy buddies. Did he change or alter his objective or his view of love? Never. Being humbled in this manner did not discourage him from seeking and achieving his goal of love and completeness.

I have often observed this kind of playful teasing in my own youthful encounters. Being rejected and being told that you "are not good enough" hurts. Loving peer caring and teasing can generate a powerful bond of closeness. In more severe forms of psychic tormenting it plants the seeds of paranoia that have a lifetime negative effect of feeling not OK, low self-esteem and depression. Freddie continued in his quest for psychic completeness, constantly proposing marriage with frequent rejections. He felt energized by our bantering about his love life.

A few years later he joyfully and proudly informed us of his matrimonial success.

What we young navy medics did not know was that many people suffer from lovesickness, that mad, erotic drive for psychic connection and completion fueled by the mysterious life force energy. I will discuss our biochemical, hormonal surging tendencies in chapter seven. You see, Freddie's fiancée, Suzie, had a desire to make love to as many people as she could. She was constantly searching for new partners. She felt connected to everyone at a primitive, sexual level. For her, changing partners was like changing uniforms.

Much of the inspiration for our mad love chatter and excitement was inspired by our movie heroines Mae Britt and Marlene Dietrich who each played the role of Lola in the movie *The Blue Angel*. Lola was someone who would fall in love easily, but never wanted to.

In the early evening, just prior to going out for a night in the town, a cluster of young medics would gather together in the ten-foot-tall echo chamber of the shower room to chant and pay homage to the goddess, Lola:

> Falling in love again, never wanted to. What am I to do?
> Can't help it. Love's always been my game. Play it how I may.
> I was made that way. Can't help it.

Lola's biological imperative was to dance and display herself. A professor, Immanuel Rath, from the local university visited the cabaret where Lola was performing. His original intent was to monitor his students' recreational behavior. Instead, he was smitten with love sickness for Lola-Lola, lost his position at the university as a result of his brute-brain driven infatuation, traveled in her dance troupe and eventually became totally mad and shamed in the process.

This love-smitten search is an energy-surging trance pattern that overtakes our body, mind and spirit, as we search and seek for this happy state of love. Finding that connection with another person is thrilling, exciting, exhilarating and mad at the same time. Any human being, who, like Professor Rath, feels intense erotic arousal experiences ultimate pleasure and eventual devastating sorrow.

> Men cluster to me like moths around a flame. And if their wings burn, I know I'm not to blame. Falling in love again, never wanted to. What am I to do? Can't help it.

REVISTING PLATO AND LOVE

During my college years' classical studies, I had read about the eternal search for beauty and its multiple psychic manifestations that Plato described in his writings. Socrates' goddess guru, Diotima, instructed him that love was the energy that kept the world together. When a person is overtaken by the heart-throbbing beauty in another person, a maddening pulsation of the life force energy surges as it alters their consciousness in a trance-like hypnotic fashion. They become distracted from their other obligations in life and obsessed in their quest for this beauty. When there is a physical and psychic bonding, lovers become connected and linked to this circular, renewing life force energy forever. Even after relationships fade or end, the feelings generated in these madly exciting encounters continue to live on in some metaphysical, everlasting psychic plane. The joyful pulsations of all lovers' hearts continue to manifest that life force energy that is always seeking to renew her beauty. Plato called this madness because it is always out of our rational control.

OUR TRANSMITTING BRAIN'S ENERGY CHANNELS

During my college and navy days I gradually became aware of competing and interacting energetic forces operating in us. The findings of Dr. Paul McLean describe our human forebrain's evolution in three major tiers: first, the *basal ganglia* colloquially called our reptilian brain since we share this structure with vertebrates, second, the emotional mammalian brain called the *limbic system,* and third, the *frontal cortical brain* network for thinking, planning and intelligence. These forebrain brain structures interact with each other in their own unique manner and have a major influence on our personality patterns and lifestyle.

So much of our life revolves around our forebrain's capacity to function. We use our frontal thinking brain to train ourselves to manage the energetic surges originating from the knot-like masses of gray matter sitting deep in our forebrain's cellar where the basal ganglia originate. These reptilian brain cells energize our neurotransmitters, motor movements, daily rituals and routines.

Another one of our frontal thinking forebrain's major tasks is to negotiate and contain our craving, sexual energy patterns that are being activated by our limbic system. These neural structures contain the smell centers that interact with clusters of nerves that relate to anxiety, memory, feeling and sexual expression. Our amygdala (anxiety) and septum (rewards/pleasure) centers are located here. Our emotional, visceral brain can be both our friend and our enemy. It can help create great excitement, pleasure and joy for us, but can also flip into acute pain and despair. Non-rational, emotional inner dialogues such as, "I suck. I'm no good. She doesn't like me. He left me for someone else," are activated from these old, primary communication, emotionally expressive networks. We struggle for words to describe and talk about our experiences, but can only use metaphors to try to explain what is happening to us and how we are feeling.

Our cerebellum that relates to our posture, muscle movements and balance, is tucked under our three-tiered forebrain. Our base brain, also called the brain stem, houses our reticular formation, the waking and sleep-activating areas. It is surrounded by the pons, a marker for sleeping and dreaming. The pons also sends signals to all parts of our nervous system. Our medulla connects our brain to our spinal cord. This network transmits our automatic, involuntary breathing, heartbeat, waking, sleeping, swallowing and sexual patterns as it sends signals up to our thalamus, a relay station in our limbic system. Our medulla also transmits and receives signals with our connecting spinal cord as it winds down to our sacral tail sitting beneath the base of our spinal cord.

Inner psychic science practitioners have described a subtle, vibrating energy field in our pelvic floor area. This spiral, circulating, bipolar energy field near the base of our spine can create exhilarating and sexually arousing energy patterns, but can also at times result in lethargic and depressive sensations. When we are feeling passionate love we often feel a chill running up our spine that activates all our brain energies, transmitting a blissful joy throughout our entire being. I can tell you that we navy medics had our own expletives and metaphors to describe these energy patterns floating around this mysterious sacral core.

So much of our time and energy is spent coping with and managing the often conflicting signals surging from these multiple-channeled energy patterns in our interactive brain networks. Our difficulty occurs when our thinking and ancestral biological brains transmit conflicting signals that make us feel anxious and confused. Our great joy is to experience love's fullness when all of our brain systems are flowing in unison and relating in harmony.

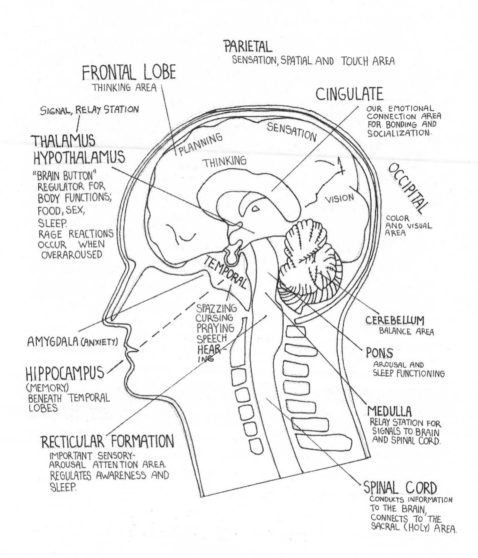

PARIETAL
SENSATION, SPATIAL AND TOUCH AREA

FRONTAL LOBE
THINKING AREA

CINGULATE
OUR EMOTIONAL
CONNECTION AREA
FOR BONDING AND
SOCIALIZATION.

SIGNAL, RELAY STATION

THALAMUS
HYPOTHALAMUS
"BRAIN BUTTON"
REGULATOR FOR
BODY FUNCTIONS;
FOOD, SEX,
SLEEP.
RAGE REACTIONS
OCCUR WHEN
OVERAROUSED

PLANNING

THINKING

SENSATION

VISION

OCCIPITAL
COLOR
AND VISUAL
AREA

TEMPORAL

SPAZZING
CURSING
PRAYING
SPEECH
HEAR-
ING

CEREBELLUM
BALANCE AREA

AMYGDALA (ANXIETY)

PONS
AROUSAL AND
SLEEP FUNCTIONING

HIPPOCAMPUS
(MEMORY)
BENEATH TEMPORAL
LOBES

MEDULLA
RELAY STATION FOR
SIGNALS TO BRAIN
AND SPINAL CORD.

RECTICULAR FORMATION
IMPORTANT SENSORY-
AROUSAL ATTENTION AREA.
REGULATES AWARENESS AND
SLEEP.

SPINAL CORD
CONDUCTS INFORMATION
TO THE BRAIN,
CONNECTS TO THE
SACRAL (HOLY) AREA.

A VIEW OF OUR BRAIN

John Twomey
NAVY MEDIC CHATTER AND LOVE SEARCHING

Riding alongside our delightful teasing each other about bodily functions lay a serious determination to learn about the physiological workings of our bodies. Our conversations about these interesting matters would move back and forth between the jocular and the serious. Sometimes our vocabulary would be very technical, that is, driven by our scientifically-oriented medical knowledge and at other times we would be cursing and swearing, manufacturing explanations and labels for the drives of our more emotionally-driven selves. I would be remiss in my description if I did not state that we were highly competitive with each other, not only in technical knowledge, but also in our love searching quests. We would work so hard and efficiently during the day, performing our duties in a serious and methodical fashion, caring for the sick and assisting all the medical staff in providing treatment and comfort for our patients. Most of us were really committed to making medical and psychological situations better. I was involved in conducting psychological exams with all branches of the military. This included checking out candidates for long-term submarine duty, as well as assessing learning problems in young children. I worked with a neurologist in evaluating memory loss and other psychological disorders and sometimes in the emergency room if a situation occurred.

At the end of our workday some of us would work out, play softball or swim at the gym. Still others would head for the nearest tavern or what we called a watering hole. Our relationship with each other would alter from being close and caring in one moment, to anger, rage and intense competition at another. When it came to dating and relationships, intense mimicking and teasing was the norm. Stealing another medic's girlfriend was not an uncommon occurrence. What seemed to be transpiring was related to which brain state was dominating our personality at that moment. In our labeling terminology it is a streaming, hormonal, energetic surge that is being activated by our asshole-driven, self-centered, old reptilian brain.

"Why do I always have to act like a wise ass? Couldn't I be nice?" was a subject that we would discuss, particularly when our day was winding down and we would be imbibing a few beers at the hospital medics' club. Those bulging bubbles of our sacral area beneath the base of our spine, colloquially referred to as our ass, have a mysterious power and energy. Young children are very tuned into this state. It is an anatomical area that is both attractive and repulsive.

Our married buddy, Tim, told us the story of his five-year-old son, Josh, who startled him in his sleep one morning as he joyfully placed his soiled undies on Tim's face and cheerily sang, "Such a sweet smell." Tim's intense rage at being subjected to such a youthful prank did not initially sit well with him. It took him days to get over the nauseous feeling that was generated by the actions of his son who had a powerful attraction to his waste products. To make matters somewhat worse our fellow medic, Lee, could not restrain himself whenever the opportunity to use the S word presented itself. One morning at breakfast a wide grin spread over his face as he informed us that we were eating "shit on a shingle." That is, chipped beef on toast. The manner in which he would sarcastically invoke this shit mantra would reverberate right through our sacral core area as a joyous smile began to overtake whatever thoughts were playing in our heads. Did not St. Augustine fondly tell us, *"Inter faeces et urinam nascimur."* (We are born amid shit and piss).

It seems that a nature-driven, cosmic laughter, so present and active in the minds and play of children, fades and recedes in the maturation process, but never really disappears from our awareness. We adults, in some fashion, also keep hold of our attraction to this biological phenomenon.

It would be just a few years later when I would be

teaching the nitrogen cycle to my high school biology class and introducing the terms feces and defecation for the flow and recycling of waste products. One of the wiseass students blurted out, "Why can't we just say shit?" I politely answered, "Your word elicits an unpleasant olfactory sensation. When you use a scientific term you can activate the more rational area of your brain and shut down that sometimes overwhelming, unpleasant, putrid reaction." The whole class laughed. We both had made our point.

Jumping ahead thirty years later, my young son and his friends would admire the charms of a beautiful young lady by saying, "She's the shit." What is your take on the meaning of this S word?

In Hospital Corps School we learned about the clusters of nerves and muscles that sit beneath our buttocks that travel right out of the sacral area into the nerves that join up with the urinary and sex centers. As we learn to tense and relax these muscles we master and tune into the subtle, energetic, sensual sensations being transmitted from our pelvic body floor. Most families have their private vocabulary for this psycho-energetic anatomical area. Buttocks, rectum or anus are the cognitive intellectual terms. In order to experience all the subtle brain energies elicited by this primal orifice, words such as bottom, backside, fanny, butt, buns and tush are used. These words invoke a smirk across our face, which is naturally being generated by our emotional brain. When spoken in a joyful manner, there is nothing more jocular than to be greeted this way, since all our brain energies are authentically expressed in this process. Even very religious people have a propensity to relate to this area of their body. The renowned religious reformer, Martin Luther, experienced divine inspiration while he was sitting on the toilet high at the top of his monastery in Germany. It was while in the process of taking a dump (emotional brain-limbic language) or defecating (intellectual frontal-brain language)

49

that he began composing his thesis for the Reformation. He was even reputed to claim that when he broke wind the effluvial scent that emanated from his sacral area traveled straight from Germany to Rome.

We have an instinctive proclivity to employ bodily metaphors of the sacral area to describe certain people that we encounter. We medics referred to arrogant, highly intellectual beings as "horse's asses." Being told that we are "a pain in the ass" is another mode of feedback we might sometimes hear. This requires little explanation. Being referred to as a "wise ass" frequently generates a smirking, approving smile that is being activated by our emotional brain. Other expressions such as "kick ass," "get off your ass" and the ultimate insult "shove it" are also emotional limbic brain activated expressions that we all know so well.

Our delightful and engaging female medical colleagues had their own take on this behavior. They once derisively proclaimed that their supervisor, Tootsie, acted as though "the sun shines right out of her ass." She was the perfect one and all that was wonderful happened because of her. She seemed to have a special fondness for herself and loved to be admired for her fancy hairstyles, as she elegantly paraded her beauty as though she were a goddess energizing the earth. Conjecture had it that this is what she thought and would very much like others to believe.

We often would tease each other that it was because of this carnal root (crack in our ass) that we can become so excitable in one moment and so still in another. In our heart of hearts, we all love our sacral area. Unknowingly, we desire to display and share our special area with the entire world and be acknowledged as a perfect asshole. There is only one problem. *Everyone wants their ass kissed; it just so happens that it stinks.*

In chapter seven I will describe this self-involved personality pattern as I introduce you to highly self-important, entitled individuals that I playfully label as *godts*, a tendency for all of us to act as perfect assholes at certain times. The Pulitzer Prize winner, Ernest Becker, simply explained it in this manner, "We are all gods who shit."

THE PLAYFUL AND THE SERIOUS IN MATTERS OF LOVE

We navy medics' favorite chatter was discussing our love-seeking adventures. The tone of the conversation depended on whether we were in the company of our female counterparts or just other guys. Having a few beers to add flavor to the conversation was always welcome. In our bantering we created new metaphors to enliven these discussions. Remember that the term metaphor has a Greek origin, *meta*, meaning above and *pherein*, meaning to carry. In other words, a metaphor is a way of creating a mind picture to elicit a feeling and familiarity of a situation, rather than its mere literal description. In this process, something that is known and familiar is transferred onto something that is less understood, such as matters of love. This powerful confluence of intellectual and emotional brain-energies creates descriptions that become metaphors. When we are just being literal and using our intellectual mode of thinking, we can deceive ourselves into believing that something is a fact, rather than just a metaphor. This is a common problem for all of us. We get stuck and don't understand and sometimes feel confused.

During our get-togethers the question of whether the stories concerning these matters of love were an actual fact or just a fantasy (bull shit) could not be determined when we attempted to analyze them with our newly acquired scientific method of examining behavior. We came to the realization, however, that this technique of creating metaphors and dramatizing our rejections in love softened our pain and energized our desire to pursue our quest for that perfect love.

In my younger days I religiously studied the history of

baseball and discovered that the pro baseball players were quite active in their sexual pursuits and had also experienced many rejections in matters of love. Those ball players also had a penchant for drinking beer. This was a popular activity for us corpsmen as well. Cold beer took the pressure off our minds and provided comfort and grounding for philosophical discussions concerning matters of love, automobiles and sports.

"Why do people really drink beer?" I would ask. After a few incorrect answers I would inform my friends, "To pee, that is, make a seal in your bladder and hold it as long as you can before you whiz."

"What are you talking about?" I would be asked. I would tell them, "To feel that rush of a special, sweet, sensuous energy flowing throughout your mind and body as you watch your hose blessing the world with the holy liquid flowing from your miraculous joy toy."

I had this same discussion about beer drinking forty years later with over a hundred vets from the Iraq and Afghanistan War. Nothing has changed except the price of beer.

Whenever there was time for serious reflection I would listen to the inner dialogue that is always playing inside my head. That voice would sometimes set off a mood that could last for hours and even days. These subjective mood states are called qualia. In these states we feel excited sometimes and hopeless at other times. During our training seminars we also learned about the hormones and neurotransmitters that are the basic ingredients for our mood and memory states. We called this our juices. Some excite us and others calm us down. I began my lifelong quest of obtaining mastery of these juices and an understanding of what activates or triggers them so I would become a good lover, an effective human being and a productive player in the games and challenges that I would encounter in my life. Maturity is really about embarking on an investigational journey of what you are attracted to, your actions and reactions, so you can learn to modify them in order to become the person you want to be.

WHO'S THE MOTHER?

Angie's Spaz

One of my many hospital assignments was to provide assistance to our highly productive, but somewhat emotionally expressive chief clerk, Angie. She was an articulate, influential civilian employee, but would often walk out of work when she felt stressed. Angie controlled the administrative component of patient discharges and was desperately needed because she was still the most efficient worker despite her frequent emotional, often vituperative outbursts. I was assigned by the chief psychiatrist to provide assistance to her at the beginning of each workday to get her off to a good start.

Angie arrived one Monday morning in a wild mood. I sensed something was up and that I had better be ready to listen.

"Twomey, what am I doing here?"

"Working."

"For what?"

"To support your family and children."

"That's right. I work and sweat here to send my children to parochial school. My husband works hard too. What do you think one of those nuns said to my daughters?"

"What?"

"She told them that Mary is their real mother."

I gulped a silent, "Oh shit." A wild burst of anger was reflected in the face of this seething forty-four-year old. A stillness ensued.

"I'm their mother." A spaz erupted as wild screaming, banging and hollering rattled my startled being. Angie continued to express her resentment as she began throwing papers up to the ceiling and thumbing her ruler on her desk ranting," I work, cook and do everything for my children. What right does that nun have to tell my children that Mary is their mother? I'm their mother. I have to get them out of that school. These damn nuns don't know what they are saying. My kids don't love me like they used to. They talk about school and Mary their mother. What the hell is going on Twomey? Say something."

Trying to defuse some of Angie's wildness, I spoke very softly.

"You sure have a point. You really work hard to take care of your children. You sure love them. I am so sorry that you have to be put through this."

"Oh shut up Twomey. You are just as bad as those nuns."

"Come on Angie! You know I really respect what you have to say."

"Ya! Thanks Twomey." She settled down. "I've got work to do. You too. Get the hell out of here."

I left sheepishly, smiling and thinking to myself, it all depends on how you see the world. Angie's world is not a nun's world.

Such a great learning!

Suffice it to say, I finished my tour in the navy as a changed person. The camaraderie and excitement of my navy day adventures had altered my rational thinking perspective to a refreshing, global, open-minded inquiry into what is really happening in the human psyche, particularly in matters of love and relationships. Initially, I had been stunned by the melodic cursing patterns and life style of a navy medic. We slept in double bunks, had little privacy or a real personal self, and all were somewhat forced to conform to one way of doing things. The motto was, "There is the right way and the navy's way." For example, Workman, our only by-the-rules chief, would not allow my friend Tim to swap duty assignments with me so he could spend the night with his family. He denied our request, bellowing in his most authoritative tone, "If the navy wanted you to have a wife, it would have issued you one." We chuckled, did the right thing and Tim went home.

I gradually became somewhat numb to the F-sound being invoked about almost everything. The lure and manner of this musical, resonating F-sound being uniquely expressed, by so many individuals in so many different ways and situations, was intriguing to me. During my career I discovered that many other professionals were interested in this F-sound expression. Dr. Candice Pert, in her book *Molecules of Emotion*, described her mentor's reaction to her discovery of the opiate receptor: "Fuck," he said in a low voice, continuing to look at the numbers…. "Fuck, fuck, fuck," he began to sputter…his face lighting up in a wild grin." Dr. Steven Pinker, a Harvard University psychologist, also presented his views of the F-sound, in the article "What the F***?"

This F-sound constantly resonating in my mind and being invoked by almost everyone motivated my quest to explore what is beneath the surface of these primitive, energizing, expletive modes of expression and their relationship to attraction, rejection and releasing tensions in matters of love. It seems that sailors curse and swear in much the same manner as devout religious people constantly invoke God in their prayerful exhortations. I would learn later that brain-imaging studies would demonstrate that cursing, praying and swearing are generated by the same emotional brain-related neurons. In matters of love what attracts and grabs our attention is related to this pulsating, and forever reverberating, invocative and evocative energetic flow. Was this what Freud was proposing in his formulations about libidinal energy?

Chapters seven and eight will further explain my psychobiological approaches to our emotional brain-related primary communication modalities. My many navy adventures concerning matters of love that I observed and experienced would influence my teaching, research and therapeutic approaches for the rest of my professional career.

4.

THE WISDOM OF GREAT TEACHERS

Saying good-bye to all my navy friends was not difficult since I began attending school just a few miles away. Occasional Friday or Sunday social events kept our connection strong. Still, I could feel our interests slip-sliding away as I elevated my energies to exploring complex academic matters of learning, behavior change and relationships. I had developed a strong interest in studying the deep recesses of the brain during my navy days and how developmental deficiencies affect behavior and learning.

You may not know that many of us are not 100% right-handed or left-handed, but are somewhere in between. Take the test now.

1. Cover your right eye, making a cup over it with your left hand, then look out at what you see. Repeat the same exercise covering the other eye.
2. Which eye do you experience as your lead or dominant eye? This is your power eye.
3. Close your eyes. Imagine you are going to kick a soccer ball or football. What leg would you kick with? Feel the sensation. This is your lead leg.
4. What hand do you write with? What hand do you eat with? What is your dominant side when you bat, play tennis or other sport activities? Are you a straight righty, lefty or a mix? Inventory your many activities.

When you appraise this information you are tuning into how your neurons express your unique psychobiological body signature patterns. Another manner of saying it: you are observing the method by which your body, mind and brain vibrate, energize, learn and relate to the world around you. I label this behavior as being your neurokinetic expression, your primary communication and non-verbal expressive modality. This has a lot to do with how the personality patterns of our mind search for love and recognition. I will explain in great detail this mode of relating in chapter eight. Think of a dog wagging its tail. It is just part of its nature. So too, are our neurokinetic, expressive, energy display patterns as we wag, swagger or dance in our own unique style or manner. I call this our expressive energy field pattern.

In many cultures left-handed persons were considered sinister because of the way they expressed themselves. Michelangelo was an oddball lefty. In my high school days I worked in a restaurant as a counterperson. My boss, Joe Casey, demanded that I scoop ice cream right-handed. I could do it, but always used my left hand when he was not looking. One of my personal goals was to train my brain by switch-hitting in softball games and turning and breathing on both sides when swimming. My point is that we are all physically and psychically unique in our personality patterns and should not expect others to be exactly like us. In our interactions with others, especially in matters of attraction and closeness, our unique, neurokinetic, expressive, energetic interests take us into places and spaces where we may have never been before. These experiences can be exhilarating or depressing. They can be engaging. They can be confusing. As these energetic, expressive surges subside we tend to self-reflect on whether we felt nourished or drained by transactions with situations and people, particularly in matters of love.

Following my discharge from active navy duty, good fortune provided me a full time biology teaching position at South Boston High School. My days and evenings were long and intense with lots of work. I arranged my time to continue to consult with my naval hospital mentor concerning personality and psychological testing matters, as well as saying a casual hello to my medic friends. Being a highly verbal, metaphor-creating wiseass with a penchant for academic barbing, I enjoyed being a graduate student and the opportunity to explore and grow in my many areas of interest, particularly the relationships between intelligence, emotional learning and the mind. I was drawn to exploring the research findings of Bluma Zeigarnik called the Zeigarnik Effect. It simply stated that people tend to remember interrupted more than completed events, especially if there was strong emotion involved.

I loved to employ my youthful skill in memorizing baseball lineups and rosters that utilized the same emotionally-related hippocampal brain networks and learning style that I used to memorize the names and formulations of academic researchers and their findings. I was not the shy, clandestine type of student, but was willing to share my extensive navy experiential knowledge in the humble manner that my Jesuit teachers had modeled during my high school days. I was shunned by the serious intellectuals seeking hard science information and welcomed by faculty and fellow students who believed that research had to have some practical value if it was worth exploring.

The psychological relationship between stress and physical illnesses became another strong area of interest. Dr. John Gilmore was my favorite professor and eventual dissertation chairman. Our initial contact was our Socratic dialogue concerning the nature of psychological and physical illnesses. As we spent more time in seminars, a wonderful student–teacher relationship ensued. At this time, I was fortunate enough to meet up with another renowned psychologist, Dr. John Arsenian, who sparked my interest in exploring the origin of physical illnesses and unresolved emotional attachments that cause paranoid states, that is, extremely suspicious and accusative behavior.

A GREAT AWAKENING

On a rainy Sunday afternoon during the last semester of my coursework for my doctorate in psychology, I took a trip by myself to the Museum of Science in Boston. All my naval friends had been reassigned to new situations in preparation for combat. There was no one to carry on and engage in crazy navy boy razzing. To be honest, I like being alone sometimes, away from all the conversational companionship of my friends. Quiet reflections dominated my thinking as I contemplated my academic future. My mind began to match the rhythm of the staccato beat of the raindrops pounding on the museum's tin roof, spinning my attention to a multi-media exhibit of the human heart. All my regular, intellectual learning receded to the background as my own heart began to pulsate and throb with the sounds generated by the human heart display. The intonation of the narrator's voice penetrated my psyche:

One heartbeat is the product of a million synchronized cells.
The heart is the product of many individualized cells.
When heart muscles are separated, each cell has a beat of its own.
When heart muscles' cells touch, they beat at the same rate.
One heartbeat is the product of the synchronized beat of many cells.

Each of us possesses a personal heart center and desires to merge it with the universal heart through connecting with another human heart. Our cells vibrate with other cells and create a "love connection" in this psychic and physical merging. This vital force energy flows though our heart area, pulsating love in its expression of beauty, connection and completion. It is like an electrical connection with two poles that can both excite you and destroy you. We are driven by nature to follow this flow of energy and synchronize our heartbeat with our beloved. When we manifest love we surrender our individual heartbeat, psychically and physically. In this mysterious encounter of experiencing love, we experience nature's ecstatic creative flow of energy. I will review the history of this approach in chapter nine when I review approaches to explaining this mysterious energy.

I walked out of the museum with the spark of an idea to study patients who had experienced a heart attack. Professor Gilmore, and other researchers, had theorized that there was a significant correlation between a heart attack and the loss of a significant personal relationship for the patient. These physical and psychic symptoms are interrelated. This is what we call the body–mind connection. The physical heartbeat tells its own story of what the psychic heart is experiencing.

In my clinical practice as I conducted interviews with many combat veterans, I learned that they too experienced considerable coronary symptoms. A body awareness relaxation breathing technique called autogenic training, which was developed over a hundred years ago in Germany by Dr. Johann Schultz, can be an effective tool in mastering and reducing rapid heartbeat symptoms. My dissertation confirmed a significant correlation between high degrees of anxiety and hyper-vigilant suspicious behavior, with heart attacks. It was considered weird to make such a claim at this time. The Heart Association had no interest in further exploring these findings.

JUMPING TO SOUTHERN ILLINOIS UNIVERSITY: ANOTHER BEGINNING

I was heavily recruited by several universities and chose to join the faculty at Southern Illinois University. One of my former navy buddies had returned home to this area and welcomed me with his wife and small daughter. During the next three years I conducted workshops in highly funded, criminal justice training programs for probation and parole officers, as well as mental health personnel. I also taught graduate level courses in the psychology of personality and group therapy. Money for demonstration research was plentiful. There were many scholarships available for all the enrolled students. At this time, I was neither emotionally nor intellectually attuned to love matters other than my own. Assessing a person's developmental stages, learning deficiencies and devising programs that would generate change was my goal. Every day provided a different challenge. I worked one day a week at the federal penitentiary in Marion, Illinois that recently had been constructed to replace the infamous Alcatraz. I trained my students in hands-on practice interviewing sessions with the inmates. Additionally, training sessions that I was conducting in behavioral management therapy for the staff were beginning to demonstrate a transformative intervention in the quality of prison life. Being told I was a maverick for change, with vituperative outbursts from status quo individuals, was not uncommon. Competition among my peers was fierce. Theoretical battles and approaches to matters of love, the mind and behavior, were argued in the way of the intense theological debates that took place in early America.

In my university classes I postulated a person's emotional disposition often reflected the philosophical approach with which we view the mind and love. Could it be we are attracted to the sages of old, such as Hippocrates, Aristotle or Plato? Do we attempt to be as purely empirical as the schools of behaviorism purported by Wundt, Pavlov and Watson and championed by Boring's psychology department at Harvard?

John Watson had excited America with his intellectual, scientific, behavioral psychological approaches that were designed to focus only on laboratory scientific factors. His personal life was so sexually scandalous that he was terminated from his university position. He just reinvented himself and successfully promoted his methods in commercial advertising. Can practical knowledge be acquired through rigorous laboratory experiments?

Do we advocate experiential learning techniques and skills acquired from real world interactions with all its complexities, such as the Freudian, Adlerian, Jungian and Rogerian approaches promulgated by Murray and Allport in the School of Social Relations at Harvard? The same epistemological issues still exist today, but dogmatic, intellectually seductive, pseudoscientific postulations in our litigious, politically-correct society have replaced debating matters of love and the mind. There is so much isolation of factions due to each one's belief that they have the perfect approach and solution to the knotty issues related to personality and psychology. Researchers are often mixing sociological factors with psychological variables. As a result, their conclusions are more emotionally and politically value-generated, rather than being purely scientific. The nature of knowledge called epistemology is still a matter of important inquiry.

The staff attendants at the Chester Mental Health Center for the Criminally Insane tested my competence during one of the training sessions I conducted. They had primed and rehearsed a seriously disturbed felon, Jason, to convince me during an interview that he was no longer mentally ill and he would no longer assault people. I let Jason talk for about fifteen minutes. He answered all my questions very clearly and rationally, like everything was OK and he was ready for discharge. The smirks on the staff's faces were a sure signal to me that they were up to something. Out of nowhere my intuitive self took over. I was holding a piece of chalk and asked Jason the question, "If you had a large candy bar would you share it with someone?" As I said the word, *share*, I broke the chalk in half. It triggered a wild rage response in Jason.

"No one is going to have any of my candy. That's mine. Fuck you." A slew of expletives erupted. The staff was stymied. Jason was escorted out of the room. I politely said to the staff attendants, "You have your answer gentlemen." This drama won their trust in my approach in relating to severely mentally ill people.

MY ROMANCE

My brother, David, picked me up at the airport after I had just finished a two-week visit to Ireland. He had made plans to meet his fiancée at the Wursthaus for dinner. This was a landmark in Harvard Square for good food and welcoming hospitality. The scent of fine German cuisine and briny ale held a special charm for many. It was a pleasant, warm, early August evening, the air redolent with the scents of mid-summer blooming. Mother Nature was showing off the fullness of her beauty tonight, but little did I know there was a greater treat in store for me. My brother's fiancée had been shopping with a coworker and surprised us by bringing her. To my utter delight, her friend was an auburn-haired Nordic beauty.

Her gentle footsteps and charming demeanor made me speechless. Her energy was vibrating a soft, welcoming whisper. Our eyes melted into a state of oneness as the greenish-colored shade of her irises shone right through my whole being. My heart began to pulsate with joy. The pleasant chatter of our group of four was just a mask for my smitten mind. A sparkling sensation of romantic love possessed us. This was it. The wedding took place the next summer. We spent the next year living in a quaint cottage house on campus. Matrimonial bliss ruled my life.

REFINING GROUP SKILS

During my Southern Illinois University days I became enamored with the Transactional Analysis Group Therapy approach founded by Dr. Eric Berne the author of the bestselling book, *Games People Play*. This method offers both cognitive and emotional techniques that enable a person to change and alter their perspectives of themselves and how they relate to other people in their life. Berne's methods were practical, teachable and had a huge following. The only problem is that the psychological terms that this approach utilizes are metaphors.

They are not scientific but provide practical explanations and solutions for the pain and anxiety we frequently experience. For example, the term *stroking*, that is, saying hello and seeking contact and connection with people refers to one of our basic human needs. The research findings of Rene Spitz and John Bowlby scientifically demonstrated this human biological need for contact and connection.

There are many individuals who are searching for more emotional contact than a polite hello to each other. Facebook would be considered a verbal and visual stroking model of psychically touching one another. The girl in the woman, and the boy in the man have a natural curiosity to gawk and check out those with whom we come into contact. This also is related to our old brain visual and motor system's natural curiosity to expand, explore, relate and compare ourselves to others.

At the annual Transactional Analysis conference I discovered that there was more to our professional relationship when Dr. Berne's emotional brain's surging energy field took over his rational, professional composure as he began spazzing at me during a short conversation we were having on this very subject of primary communication. I listened silently, as his highly emotional brain flooded rant ran right through me. I crossed my arms as my throat gulped and my breath crunched. He abruptly walked away. I was stymied by this sudden outburst, all the while my inner self dialogue reflecting, "This guy sure has a lot of sadness."

About an hour later a composed Eric Berne approached me somewhat sheepishly as we resumed our chat. I felt we got really close because of that encounter. My inner mantra is always related to my navy day experience of, "No spaz, no closeness." I wrote articles in his journal. Our relationship was on a productive student–teacher relationship.

I frequently traveled to California to be with my colleagues who shared Dr. Berne's approach to group work. I was searching for technologies that could refine and enhance human communication techniques including biofeedback, as well as other body-centered therapeutic approaches. It sounds like a litany, but I also made the acquaintance of Fritz Perls, the founder of Gestalt therapy. He was a highly attuned, dynamic sage, who had a huge following. Expressing your resentment and connecting to your inner psychic core was what he was about. He would not let you analyze or look for causes, but rather experience your question as it relates to your own inner consciousness. When attendees at a meeting would want to theorize, Dr. Perls would immediately create a psychodramatic dialogue with the person to respond to their question by engaging themselves in an experiential self-reflection about the meaning of their question. If a person persisted, Dr. Perls would spaz, and then walk out of the room laughing at their inauthentic, defensive need to intellectualize and thereby avoid emotional contact with what was really transpiring. This primary communication mode of relating had a huge influence on me and strongly connected me to my own inner resentments in my psychic core that would become both an asset and liability for the rest of my life.

SIU days were replete with new opportunities for expanding my horizons and meeting many exciting, renowned experts. Encountering Zvi Hermon, a psychologist and the first commissioner of the Israeli prison system, had a profound influence on my career. He boldly asserted that a prison system could not rehabilitate political prisoners. One evening, just before he was scheduled to give a major university lecture, my wife had invited him to dinner at our house. I stopped at the grocery store to pick up a few items and silently stood in line. To my utter surprise and embarrassment, he motioned me to join him at the front of the checkout line. The energy he generated was assertive, but also humorous and playful. A stunned, bewildered look came over the faces of the dozen people in line as he spoke in a pseudo-apologetic tone, "I have to give a lecture tonight and I am so excited that I am going to get a home-cooked meal. I haven't been home in weeks."

I paid my bill and was sheepishly walking out of the store with this ordinary, middle-aged, somewhat short, slightly bearded man. As the customers continued to gawk at us, out of nowhere he thunderously roared, "Don't worry. I have been fully analyzed." My mood of shyness and embarrassment evaporated into delighted laughter.

The events of the evening were a huge success. Zvi was invited for an extended stay at the university. He taught me so much about hypnosis and psychotherapy and, at the same time, shared with me many stories of love and how sensual his native language of German was for him. I have never been the same since his weeklong visit.

SIU provided so many energetically elevating experiences that I shared with fellow friends, colleagues and students. There was financial support for many research and demonstration projects. My department provided me funding for many training programs in organizational development, group dynamics and community psychology. This staff development funding enhanced my skills in providing training in human relations for probation and police officers, all with the expectation of reducing crime and delinquency. This era of generous funding, however, would soon come to an end. I began to grow weary of traveling the entire country and at the same time teaching university classes and writing training manuals. My many educative and transformative leanings at SIU were ready to be tested and played out in East Coast academic and clinical settings.

RETURN TO BOSTON

During one of my traveling forays to Boston, I learned that there was an opening at the local VA clinic. I knew all about this facility from my navy days. They were in the process of creating new staff to deal with the Vietnam War vets. I was hired because of my human relations group psychology skills. My goal was to professionally refine my in-depth psychodynamic skills. I hoped to learn from their highly experienced staff that had many more years of clinical experience than me. The sharing of cases and training provided an outstanding reorientation to intense therapeutic practices. My plan was to work there for a short while and then resume college teaching.

I had lots of energy and my professional life was very busy since my approach was as a New Age, West Coast type of group therapist. The old norm of passive listening at a distance was being replaced with an active, collaborative participant observer model. I conducted demonstration workshops in group dynamics for the faculty at Harvard Business School, the Massachusetts Psychological Center and several hospitals and organizations. Serving on the steering committee for the soon to be founded Massachusetts School of Professional Psychology provided me with the opportunity to network with fellow professionals. It was also rewarding to work as a project consultant and group leader with thirteen-year-old school children in a newly funded Project Adventure program. The findings indicated that most pre-adolescents prefer to engage in activities such as climbing ropes and bouncing on trampolines, rather than verbally sharing their emotional reactions to what they were experiencing.

My academic interest centered on exploring our thinking and expressive patterns, particularly how our feelings influence our thinking and behavior in a group setting. (I now know that the only person who seems to be free of emotion is Siri. She is the iPhone voice, completely information-oriented, never irritated and does not have an emotional brain influencing her information processing.)

During the many group sessions that I facilitated, I observed that the more emotionally engaged that the members were with each other as they participated in the group process, they would eventually stop speaking to each other and just slide into a silent mode of relating. My term for this behavioral state is "the world without words." This non-talking interval can last for long periods of time. The first person that speaks after the group has sat silently often became the target for angry outbursts from other members of the group. Communicating just with words without feelings can generate anger and competition in the group, especially as attraction and leadership issues begin to emerge. I attempted to scientifically investigate these group dynamics processes but discovered that my findings and explanations were just metaphors and could not be stated in scientific terms.

During this time I had many opportunities to interact with the neuroscience pioneer Dr. Frank Schmidt who was my wife's godfather. He straightened me out more than once about these epistemological psychological formulations. Of course he was correct. There are no scientific methods or instruments available to measure this behavior since its origins are at a non-verbal primary communication level. Dr. Schmidt was a colleague and close friend of my father-in-law who was chairman of the biology department and eventually was promoted to be the dean of science at MIT.

One of my major career goals was to become a skilled psychotherapist and understand the nature of the mind. I chose to work at a facility that had highly skilled mentors who could enrich my clinical skills. The voices of Drs. John (Jock) Murray, Peter Sifneos and Morris Adler still reverberate in my brain. What you can and cannot do to effectively help somebody was their principal theme. These psychiatrists all had served in the military and had considerable experience in treating veterans' issues, particularly their nightmares, flashbacks and matters of love.

Dr. Jock, who was my mentors for eight years, served

as a colonel in the Army Air Force during World War II. He frequently discussed our emotional brain driven reactions to situations when individuals feel they are mistreated or misunderstood. They become emotionally flooded and react with intense rage and anger. Their old self-serving reptilian brain energy patterns interfere with their thinking self and so they are not able to observe how their behavior is affecting other persons. They spaz and then attribute the problem to another person or situation. Their self-serving mind takes over as they relive their perceived mistreatment. A grudge soon follows. Dr. Jock labeled this personality pattern as *narcissistic entitlement.*

Dr. Jock was a personal friend of President Dwight D. Eisenhower's physician, Dr. Howard Snyder. Most everyone fondly referred to Eisenhower as Ike. All three men would often get together for lunch in Boston. Dr. Jock told me all about his role in treating Ike's heart attack that occurred at his Washington golf course one afternoon. Dr. Jock had to fly to Washington to assist Dr. Snyder in managing the crisis. Ike was known for his temper and intense emotional reactions to stressful situations. It seems he had informed everyone that he was not feeling well and did not want to be disturbed. There were, however, disputes at the White House that had to be resolved. Ike had to stop playing golf and ride a buggy to the club house to take the phone call. He blew up in a rage and soon thereafter had a heart attack.

Dr. Jock had been a New Hampshire country doctor before he traveled to Austria to study with Freud. Dr. Jock arranged for Ike's wife Mamie to lie down beside him in his bed. Dr. Jock was practicing his country doctor methods so that Mamie could behave for Ike as though matters were not that serious. Everyone was fearful that Ike would erupt emotionally again. He made a satisfactory recovery. In retrospect, Ike had many posttraumatic stress disorder symptoms that I will discuss in chapter eleven. In fact, Eisenhower had choice expletives for Dr. Jock every time he saw him.

Dr. Peter Sifneos was my supervisory consultant for three years. He was a Harvard professor and considered to be a pioneer in the field of short-term psychodynamic therapy. Assessing anxiety, intelligence and coping skill levels was a major determining factor in a successful psychotherapy outcome. I can still hear his voice in my head telling me what to do and not to do in my professional work. Peter used the word, time, in almost every sentence he spoke. My favorite conversation with Peter was when he shared his experiences about a major symposium held in London on the role of learning in psychotherapy sponsored by the CIBA Foundation. All the major experts in the field of therapy presented their papers and approaches to treatments. During the first four days, there was little collaborative interaction among the participants. They all seemed to be guarded and severely critical of anyone else's approach. On the last day of the conference, the experts did agree on one matter: it takes time to get to know your patient. A few years later CIBA released a major publication on the proceedings. As I read the book that my father-in-law had received, and passed on to me, I chuckled recalling Peter's story. I affectionately refer to Peter as Dr. Time.

Dr. Morris Adler and I met twice a week for nine months in a psychotherapy seminar. He was the first chief of psychiatry at our clinic that had been founded after the end of World War II. His intuitive, therapeutic approach stated that a therapist has to empathically tune into the patient's disease and emotional energy field. Eventually, through engaging empathic contact, the therapist acquires the disease in a mild form. This manner of relating provides the patient with the capacity to recover, heal and acquire an improved sense of self. I can attest that this was my situation in working with the severely mentally ill. I had to work my way out of the depressing energy that my patients were transmitting. It is not a pleasant situation or feeling, but when my normal self resurfaced I was psychically strong and able to effectively relate to very severely disturbed patients.

During Dr. Adler's seminar, one doctor presented the case of his combat Vietnam patient who broke furniture in his office during a therapy session. Dr. Adler requested that this doctor ask his patient if he had killed women and children in Vietnam. During his next session the doctor asked that question. The patient acknowledged this was what was bothering him, but could not tolerate his unbearable anxiety and asked for a break from treatment to think things over. This same phenomenon exists today. Many people cannot handle the shame, guilt and self-destructive thoughts that are streaming in their consciousness. The theoretical, rationally-oriented therapists asked Dr. Adler what his evidence was to make such a supposition. His answer was there is always another level transpiring and it is the therapist's task to tune into the patient's thought process and inner mind and help the patient express what they are thinking and experiencing.

Dr. Adler died suddenly. We all mourned the loss of his charisma and inner psychic access to what happens between the therapist and patient. His major focus was for psychotherapists to carefully examine the feelings that they experienced while they were meeting with their patients. He was my hero. I modeled myself on his methods and in his memory made a presentation on his approach to treatment at our clinic grand rounds.

During this period there were many psychotherapy seminars designed to address the problems, anomie and rejection that returning Vietnam vets were experiencing. The media had sensationalized these problems, as increased political pressure demanded that something be done to help these vets. I was assigned to be a community outreach worker. Since I was a veteran I could establish rapport and relate with many of these maligned heroes. I participated in media-driven workshops for these vets who did not view themselves as having psychiatric problems, just as mistreated and misunderstood.

During one of our psychotherapy seminars, a colleague reported undocumented findings about a "truth serum," sodium pentothal, which was used in experimental interviews to help vets identify their trauma. It seemed that some of them killed themselves after undergoing this treatment. Just because a person identifies what happened or what they experienced does not mean the problem is solved. As a matter of fact, it can make things worse. Things have not changed too much today. Vets run away from what is bothering them. It is too painful.

Love and Mental Illness: A Tutorial with Dr. Elvin Semrad

I had heard a great deal about Dr. Elvin Semrad, a highly respected Harvard psychiatrist, from many fellow students during graduate school days. He was considered to be the master in treating severe mental illness and was scheduled to consult at rounds at our clinic one Wednesday morning. At that time there were no clinicians who were willing to be embarrassed and present a case in which Dr. Semrad would interview their patient. I volunteered to be the presenter to this elderly, robust psychiatrist who had the unique gift of being able to relate to severely ill patients and enable them to contact their heart-related love pain. He would speak in a soft, yet confronting tone, as he would probe the patients to talk about their failed romances. Then he would mildly exhort them to begin searching for love again. It seemed as though he was just pressing a button to reset their psyches to resume a lost quest.

I had been working with a forty-year-old patient, Nick, who was very tuned into voices in his head and sounds in the environment. Our initial meeting was spent discussing the spelling of my last name, which ends in "y." He reported to me that his previous doctors were always asking him, "Why? Why?"

I told him I would never ask "Why?" but sometimes, "How come?" Mentally ill patients often are very literal and have trouble with metaphors. Nick was no exception. We shared an interest in radios. This common connection served as a reality check when we would explore other psychic areas of his life. Over time, his symptoms became less severe and his life more stabilized. There were forty mental health practitioners present, not so much to hear about me, but to watch Dr. Semrad interview my patient. I presented my case for about twenty minutes and then Dr. Semrad examined the patient. He usually interviewed the patient for about fifteen minutes. Matters were flowing smoothly, when out of nowhere, Dr. Semrad changed his focus and asked my patient whether he had been in love.

"Where is he going with this?" I worried. The entire tone and energy of the dialogue erupted from blandness to an animated discussion of the patient's long lost love of twenty years ago just prior to his breakdown. The pain that the patient felt following his rejection was resurrected. The patient's entire facial expression and body posture changed as repressed emotional energies surfaced. The interview ended with Dr. Semrad instructing the patient to talk with me about this event. We did this over the next year. This voice-hearing, seriously impaired patient started to release his symptoms through coughing as he began to emote and feel his psychic pain. He simultaneously complained about intense physical pain in his chest and heart area. Dr. Semrad's gentle voice introducing matters of love with Nick, and Nick's response, was enough to make me alter my focus in working with people.

This loss of experiencing love and its resulting emotional contact, with no awareness of its origins in terms of what has taken place in the patient's life, is a dreaded syndrome. It is so painful. The mind's emotions become flat and still. The disappointed heart melts and disappears into nothingness as it flees from its throbbing anguish. Depression sets in. Inner persecutory voices replace the conversation of the real world. Can we help people with these difficulties? Can we release archaic tensions from the past?

A plan was initiated for Nick to focus on reality issues as the voices in his head began to recede. His pain began to diminish and he no longer experienced confusing, inner psychic conflict in his everyday life. He stopped talking about radios and began to collaborate with me in the quest to change his lifestyle and search for a new love. He began a relationship with a woman his age. Within a year he established a new life and moved to another town. He no longer needed me. He was on his own.

Individuals such as Nick who have intense bodily symptoms are frequently unable to release tension and require medication to enable them to acquire emotional neutralization and containment skills. This treatment is necessary because the organism is vibrating so excessively that as a result psychic agitation overwhelms us. Emotional stabilization techniques that consist of specialized body awareness and breathing exercises such as the circle breathe exercise can help alter and diminish this powerful, possessive, life-crippling love anxiety.

I continued relating to Dr. Semrad throughout the remaining short years of his life. His sincerity, humility and astute caring in treating the mentally ill left a profound effect on me. So much so I began talking a lot about love during my group therapy sessions with severely ill patients. Most groups ended with us singing the song:

> Be sure it's true when you say I love you,
> It's a sin to tell a lie.
> Millions of hearts have been broken
> Just because these words were spoken
>
> I love you, yes I do, I love you.
> If you break my heart I'll die. So be sure it's true when you
> say I love you.
> It's a sin to tell a lie
>
> "It's a Sin to Tell a Lie", by Billy Mayhew

We would all joyously laugh, as the group ended on a high

note.

Not all situations are the same. In a more problem-solving focused group for younger patients we often discussed love, dating and relationships. A situation arose in which I had to deal with a serious behavior problem that my patient, Lars, presented.

LARS:
MANAGING LOVE SURGING BASE BRAIN INDUCED MADNESS

Lars was a handsome, slim, twenty-six-year old who had a strong interest in love and beauty from his earliest years. His piercing, Scandinavian-blue eyes, soft-spoken voice and gentle demeanor rarely went unnoticed as he engaged in his daily interactions with people. In group therapy he liked to converse and philosophize about political matters, but avoided any involvement in discussions of sporting events. He would withdraw into himself if the conversations were not to his liking. When surging emotional matters intruded into his consciousness during the group, he would display a shy and sullen stupor. When he did speak, a lonely feeling and the wish to be in some other place always lurked in the background of his voice.

Lars left home after high school and enrolled in a Lutheran college in a nearby state. For the first six months he did quite well, both socially and academically, but eventually he became overwhelmed with a sad and lonely feeling. His grades remained acceptable, but he was asked to leave the school because his behavior in the library was becoming upsetting to the young female students. He would sit in a provocative posture displaying his crotch while pretending to study, when he was really attempting to provoke a reaction and receive attention from his female classmates. Lars returned home unhappy, sullen and disappointed that he was not moving forward in his life. He worked for a few years in his father's business and eventually sought treatment for depression.

In our sessions he revealed that during his younger years mom and dad would take him to bed with them each evening. They would hug and cuddle him. He felt so adored and loved. This special nighttime ritual continued into his middle school years. The warmth and comfort he had felt was something so wonderful that it was hard to forget. He continues to pine for this idyllic excitement and comfort. This early interaction with his parents affected his emotional maturation. Eventually he developed a propensity to show himself off by displaying a clothes-on erection, as he would yearn for a special physical connection with women. Lars' fellow group therapy patients labeled this, in slang emotional brain terms, "donkering."

An incident occurred sometime after we had begun meeting. One evening, to the surprise of his thinking self, Lars found himself in a booth at a city strip club cuddling up with the alluring female practitioners. He savored their scent and loving, nurturing words. He bought them several drinks and at the end of the evening he was shocked to discover that he had run up a five hundred dollar bill. He hastily paid the bill with his credit card. Within the next hour, rage and fury overtook his mind as shock at the amount of money that he had spent set in. He immediately called the credit card company to say that his card had been stolen earlier in the day. He was successful in this manufactured fiction and the charges were deleted. He was elated that he did not have to pay for his errant behavior. His anxiety dissipated. He felt that this club should not have taken advantage of him.

About a month later the remembered excitement of this experience was so arousing that he found himself at another club dancing and flirting with the beautiful dancing ladies. The resulting seven hundred dollar credit card bill made him very anxious and soon thereafter he requested an emergency meeting with me. I told him that his previous story would not work this time and asked what he would like to do to modify his behavior. He was at a loss to explain the sensuous arousal that drew him to these strip joints and did not know how to manage his urges.

In just a week, matters became a little more complicated and immediate when he donkered, that is, exhibited his aroused self to a female passenger who was sitting next to him on the commuter train. She immediately pressed charges. After some legal negotiating that included Lars agreeing to treatment for his behavior, I directed him to wear a cupped jock strap when he traveled to and from work.

Lars was not pleased with my prescriptive behavioral intervention, but reluctantly complied. He became sullen, sad, and angry with me and blamed me for his poor quality of life. He sneered at me for many months. Our treatment focus was directed primarily towards helping him to contain his surging sexual drive and to think with his rational brain when his donkering impulses arose. After an extended period of treatment, Lars acquired skills that enabled him to activate his thinking self and contain his base brain, surging, primitive sexual energy.

The great neurologist, Hughlings Jackson, proposed that these surging, archaic brain energy fields need to be dampened and contained in order for human beings to transact and behave in a society. In our present day's mind-body psychoneurological (mind–brain), oriented approach we must train ourselves to master these reptilian brain-based erotic, luring, infusing energy patterns, the neurotransmitters and hormones being activated from the deep recess of our non-thinking brain. Remember in my navy medic days we playfully dubbed these scientific constructs *juices* in our attempts to create metaphors to describe our own experiences of the wild young male surging from our own base brain.

During my adolescence I wondered whether I was running my life or whether the hormonal sexual surges were running me. Gradually, frontal brain intellectual control became the dominant director of my wildly surging mind. Not far below, however, lies our ever-present inner psychic desire to express our creative love searching nature; the life force and love's desire for physical expression are just oozing and lurking in the background, awaiting their opportunity to manifest themselves when we least expect it. This phenomenon was demonstrated scientifically during magnetic imaging studies when lovers were asked to describe the feelings they experienced as this psychic love was surging. Areas of the emotional limbic and archaic striped basal ganglia brain would light up. As adolescents gradually master the intensity of their surging emotional brain they are able to participate in the beauty of this process without jeopardizing the rational goals and purposeful direction of their lives.

In closing this chapter, I would like to thank you for reading my whirlwind encounters and adventures of my twenties and early thirties. Searching for answers to the meaning of life was my quest. Each individual's unique neurokinetic, energetic signature expression of growing, finding, and staying in love, makes life worthwhile and a challenge.

5.

DR. MARVIN'S OFFICE

After moving forward from my navy career I continued to explore the relationship of the body and the mind. I was rather stunned and somewhat confused when I learned that memories of past uncomfortable events are not only stored in our brains, but also strongly affect our anatomy and physiology. I then began to research the long history of these body–mind relationships that I discuss in chapter nine. My quest was to acquire the tools and techniques that would realign our body structures, release negative tensions and so elevate our energy patterns. During my time at Southern Illinois University I received a lesson in the Alexander Technique from my future teacher Dr. Frank Pierce Jones. This body realignment technique balances a person's energetic patterns. It does wonders for both our posture and our breathing. Actors, dancers and singers have found it very helpful in enhancing their artistic expression. During our training sessions Frank would direct me to focus my attention by repeating to myself, "My neck is free so my head can come forward and out."

Next I began to study a body energizing technique called Bioenergetic Analysis with Dr. Alexander Lowen. He had been a student of the infamous Wilhelm Reich, an associate of Freud, who had introduced the world to the Body Oriented Therapies. Reich was prosecuted and imprisoned by the federal government for unscientific claims about one of his inventions called an orgone box.

My teacher, Dr. Jock Murray, had examined him while he was in the federal penitentiary in Connecticut. He diagnosed him as a severe paranoid schizophrenic. Reich had become delusional about his belief that he had created a scientific discovery that would generate energy. Today we would laugh at both the madness and the seriousness of such pompous claims. This was really no different than Anton Mesmer's situation in the days of Ben Franklin. This is discussed further in the chapter on trance and the origin of hypnosis.

Another behavioral enhancement technique was called Rolfing. This muscle and tension release course of instruction realigns your whole body. It was then the in thing to experience. I personally did not like the soreness of the intense muscle massage and structural realignment that I had experienced. I thought there was a better way to do things. A college friend had been teaching me yogic postures for many years. This approach was soothing, relaxing and healing. He was way ahead of us all in terms of generating healing energy. So, of course the stars of Hollywood brought him to California to teach them.

The word was out among us body–mind explorers about Dr. Marvin, an osteopathic physician. He was one of the first students of Ida Rolf, a pioneer in realigning body tissue. Many professional athletes would consult with him for their back, shoulder and hip problems. It was said that Ted Williams had paid him a visit, for this guy knew his stuff. He could put the body and mind together. I was rather intrigued to meet with him and called for an appointment. He said, "Come in anytime," and hung up. That was different.

Running around the local Cleveland Circle Reservoir and being greeted by the musical sounds of the ducks and Canada geese, not to mention the scent of my favorite flower the yellow jonquil, was a great way to start this spring time day. "I'm going to check out this guy," was the music playing in my head and tickling my pumping heart in rhythm with my footsteps. A few hours later I arrived, rang the bell and walked in.

Dr. Marvin was sitting at his desk. He was short and unimposing, and apparently had dressed hastily and without attention. He wore no shoes or socks. He was certainly not what I had expected. He did not look like the powerful, athletic jock that I had imaged, but more like the quiet, frail monks that I had encountered when visiting monasteries. An unusual musty ether-like scent enveloped his office space. I wondered if there was some experimental research being conducted there.

It was about 9AM. I sat in a chair and began to tell him about my fluctuating energy levels, my confusion and the agitation that I would often experience, particularly after working with severely mentally ill patients. He said nothing. I couldn't tell if he was even listening to a word I said. I could feel the energy in the room starting to spin. He looked at me for a few seconds, as if something drastic was about to happen. It did. He fell to the floor with a thump, muttering with a soft hoarse tone, "All you fuckin' therapists think you know something."

I was stunned, bewildered, confused. "What did I do to get myself into this? What is going on here? What kind of act is this, what is this asshole up to?" Part of me wanted to yell, another to get out. I sat in my chair in silent bewilderment and stillness. Everything inside me stopped. It was like my breath was taken out of me in the same way that Frankie described his bodily sensations after he was shot and bleeding to death. I still, to this day, do not know what overtook me as I found myself on the floor passed out beside him.

Two hours later I emerged from this stupor-like state. As we sat on the floor Dr. Marvin still seemed to be off in another plane of existence, but at the same time his gaze was somewhat directed towards me. As he spoke his tone held the same softness, but took on an added animation and enthusiasm for his work.

"Now you found out what goes on here. When you figure it out, let me know. You're in this world alone. That's what's going on here. Just deal with what's happening with you. Find your connections and explore the energy of what's going on in your body. We rely on contributions to keep this project going."

I left his office about noon, full of excitement. I felt free, liberated, but also angry that I no longer thought of myself as a smart, knowledgeable practitioner of psychology. It was like I was young, old and nothing at the same time. In a few hours, my routine ways of relating to the world took over my energy patterns as I slid into my normal ways of seeing things. It seemed that way, but not really. My inner self-talk continued to ruminate about this non-verbal magical madness and energetic infusion.

I waited seven or eight months until I paid Dr. Marvin another visit. I dropped in on a Friday afternoon a few days before New Year's. It was grey, dark and dull outside with chilly days of icy snow reminding me that environmental factors have a major effect on people's energy. That is why societies love the holidays in order to evade the dismal strains of winter. There were no birds chirping, just a few squirrels emerging from their winter hideaways to forage. Knowing the drill, I walked right in. Dr. Marvin still spoke in his bland tone and muttered with a seemingly welcoming glimmer in his eyes, "I've been waiting for you."

I had nothing to say. The energy present was so different. It was dull. It appeared Dr. Marvin was wearing the same clothes. He was sitting on the floor. He immediately changed as he began to look as though he belonged in a psychiatric ward. His posture became stiff, his face like a corpse. He looked like he had transformed himself into an acetic, frail monk engaged in mystical contemplation. Thoughts ran through my mind, "What in hell is going on here? What is he up to today? Why am I attracted to this madness?" No sooner had these thoughts arisen than they disappeared quickly. Stillness overtook my awareness as I slowly slid into a peaceful state with him for almost an hour. "Something is going on here that I don't know anything about," was my take as we emerged from this strange manner of relating without words. He invited me to meet with his group any Saturday afternoon when I felt like it; no hurry, no pressure, just a casual get together.

John Twomey
LOVE SEARCHING AND SURROGATE SEXUAL THERAPY

I was very active in my profession during these days. I was attending regular professional meetings and was attempting to standardize treatments for anxiety, depression, and serious mental illnesses. I learned from Dr. John Arsenian, a master therapist with over forty years experience, to relate to people as people, even if they had a serious illness. They were capable of reciprocity of some kind in human relationships. My colleagues and I took large groups of severely ill patients on five-day overnight trips, frequently by air. We did things that were considered risky and potentially unmanageable. During this time I was also conducting seminars for young college students on working with the severely mentally ill. Their views and visions of healing people were not bound by the rigorous guidelines of present day therapeutic contact.

Our therapeutic center had enrolled over twenty students from the local colleges. Most were psychology majors in their senior year. They participated in community activities such as bowling, gym work, swimming and picnics with our patients. They were, in fact, contemporaries of most of our patients and were dealing with similar issues of dating and acquiring confidence in their own social interactions. Group discussions concerning dating, romance, relationships and all the intricacies of love were frequent topics. What to wear, how to say hello and meet other people were the norm. Patients were not encouraged to share their deep fears, dread of doom and gloom and other morbid stories in these groups. Those matters were reserved for professionals. Most of the discussion was positive and could get very exciting from time to time. Because one has mental illness does not prohibit or deter a quest for physical relationships. Pheromones and hormonal surges were evident in this playful, but therapeutic, process.

Two young, bright and articulate students, named Terri

and Jenny, were among the many students attending my weekly seminar that was designed to process the therapeutic issues that transpired among the student and patient members. Most of the patient members were male. Most of the students were female. When a male patient asked Terri out for a date she responded with the comment, "You're going to ask me out and you don't shave and comb your hair. Who do you think I am?" This got her patient going in the right direction. He improved his hygiene and was politely told by Terri that dating her was not the way to go. She was already in a relationship.

The subject of love and relationships was discussed at length at this weekly seminar. Jenny challenged my admonition concerning personal, intimate relations with the young men. She was a tall, attractive, college senior, training as an activity therapist at the clinic. She loved to brag about the lifestyle and open spaces of her home state of Texas. Jenny was a gifted athlete and loved to play softball with the patients. They loved to engage with her on the ball field. She demanded that they swing the bat hard when she pitched to them and loved to curse with the S-word when she made an out. Jenny did not acknowledge the traditional boundaries that were expected between her and male patients. Unbeknownst to many of us, she secretly had her own prescriptive method for helping the young men in the program. She selectively chose which ones would spend time away with her. There were no laws or statutes about sexual engagements in those days.

Sexuality was rampant in the pre-herpes and HIV days. Sexual surrogate therapy was being offered by one of the psychology practitioners in Boston. I could tell you about other pseudo-therapeutic treatments in vogue at that time, but you would not believe it. When I became aware of what was happening I frequently admonished Jenny and our patients about the unhappy disappointments and consequences of their behavior. During our sessions the group adapted my playful metaphor of baseball to describe this recreational activity. This mildly humorous approach helped ease the tension for the young patients and students who were in their twenties and seeking relationships. They did not seem to care about the consequences of their behavior and others' reactions to it, in spite of the professional guidance that was offered to them.

Chauncey was a sad-looking young lad who was a participant in this very engaging psychiatric treatment program for emotionally ill patients. His face was pale. His sorrowful eyes were most often cast downward at the floor. He stood five-foot-ten with a slender frame and gently sloped shoulders. He was always very well-dressed in comfortable, casual clothes, usually neatly pressed khakis and sneakers. He rarely engaged in conversations. The forlorn look on his face appeared to be crying out for someone to rescue him from his lonely, sad, isolated self. He would sit in a chair gawking and fix his eyes on the young, attractive, highly energized female college students who were training at the facility.

When Chauncey's gaze was acknowledged by one of the girls, usually with a warm smile or a flick of the eye, a rosy blush would spread over his pale sorrow-filled face. He would radiate with a pleasant glow for a few seconds. Then his features would realign in their habitual pattern of sadness and sullenness.

In his therapeutic groups, Chauncey was not one to disguise his strong desire for love and affection, particularly for Jenny. His passive yearning for connection screamed without sound. When he did speak he reported how unsuccessful his romantic pursuits had been. He had experienced a number of rejections in his love searching quests. His treasured belief was that love would cure all of his problems. He had been referred to our program by mental health professionals who thought that he needed community socialization experiences.

As much as one can make rules or guidelines, they are ignored in matters of love and sexual attraction. It seems that

Jenny viewed herself as someone who liked to interact and engage at many levels. Her intuitive self reflected her image of a fascinating, attractive goddess providing healing energy to the world. On the basis of her physical attributes and positive, but removed, grandiose attitude, she believed that she could solve and cure any problem. Any confrontation from the leader or other group members was ignored. Her primal energy defied a rational, reality-oriented explanation. She was not shy in expressing her interactive approach. "What they need to do is spend some time with me. They will feel much better and develop other relationships."

Chauncey felt a strong attraction to Jenny. He would always blush when in her presence. He made no secret of his rapid heartbeat and the excitement he felt for this young, energetic, arousing goddess. The other patients were very aware of Chauncey's pining for Jenny. This issue was discussed frequently at staff meetings. Some of the staff demanded that Jenny be terminated from the program. There was no agreement as to how to proceed.

"What would it be like for you to get close to her and then get dumped?" I often asked Chauncey.

"I don't care," was his regular response.

"He knows what I'm about," retorted Jenny when confronted with her behavior and the situation.

Soon after Jenny's college graduation the couple spent a weekend in romantic bliss. Chauncey did not report this event until Jenny had left town and returned to Texas.

"That was the best thing that ever happened in my life. You people don't know what you are talking about. I feel whole, happy. I don't think I need to come here any more. I can smile. Fuck you, Dr. T. You just read books."

Jenny returned to her home in Texas. Chauncey continued in the program. He felt better for a while, the usual six weeks of excitement before moods return to baseline. He thought about Jenny and frequently talked about her with a faint smile, but knew and remembered her words cautioning him that this coming together was for that weekend only. He was just one of her many loves. She had made a strong impression on him that this was no romance on her part. She was just doing what she felt in her instincts was the proper therapeutic behavior to make him whole and a happier person for that time, place and situation. Their transient encounter became a pleasant, comforting memory for Chauncey as he resumed his dominant personality characteristics of sullenness and sadness. In this sullen state one sits, sucks and sulks, as a method for comforting oneself. Chauncey was no exception. When I would call him on this mood he would smile and acknowledge it.

What was this love madness that transpired between Jenny and Chauncey? What kind of image did Jenny have of herself and her interactions with the staff and Chauncey? Where did her confidence come from? Did she believe that her therapeutic sexual treatment would really improve Chauncey's quality of life? Jenny's normal, thinking self was usurped by her emotional brain-driven psychic energy fields that led her to defy both reason and mental health norms. Her behavior can be aptly described by the Greek goddess energy *ate*, the sexual, expressive, madness that overtakes the consciousness of people and drives them into sexual situations that defy reasonable thinking. These arousing eruptions surge from deep areas of the emotional and base brain and can lead us to destinations unforeseen.

It is very interesting to note that Jenny's therapeutic methods were the same cures proposed by the ancient Greek, Roman and Arabic healers 2500 years ago. In those days it was considered a prescriptive method for healing love-sickness and love searching. I will elaborate on these ancient healing methods concerning matters of love in chapter nine. This story of Chauncey and Jenny is just one example of the real life drama that came out of these therapeutic group sessions. I would often bring the emotional exhaustion and depletion that these young patients engendered to Dr. Marvin and the office where I could find a respite to recycle and recharge my energy.

RETURN TO DR MARVIN'S

As spring was approaching I began to feel the same energy that initially drew me to visit Dr. Marvin's office. Located in a quiet section of town, it had a traditional doctor's consulting room with a desk and examining table. Three stately arched windows letting in brilliant, energizing sunlight framed the adjoining room. A pale pearl-blue rug covered almost the entire oak floor. I chatted with a few of Dr. Marvin's loyal followers who welcomed me and shared his approaches. He had trained in osteopathic medicine and had a very active practice. While performing his medical body manipulation therapy he began to observe that his patients' symptoms were being energetically transmitted to his body. He often would immediately experience their energy fields, sometimes for days. Eventually he concluded that constantly adjusting his patients' body alignment did not achieve the treatment outcome that he expected. Individuals need to take responsibility for themselves and be active participants in their own healing processes.

Dr. Marvin had assembled a number of his former patients and began a community for healing, personal growth and self-actualization. I joined the group. There were no rules. Just contact your energy patterns. Live your life your way. Couples were having babies. Gatherings were wonderful. I was on the outside of the inner circle and never felt drawn to give up my life or role in my professional and personal world. I was still teaching, practicing, going to the gym and attending to other professional matters. Yet I was different. I was paying a lot of attention to what was happening around me. I thoroughly enjoyed lying on his office floor and training myself to observe my body–mind energy flowing through me. I felt strong, powerful, weak and stubborn at the same time.

It was here on this blue rug that I would sit with Dr. Marvin for awhile and all of a sudden out of nowhere float into that unique quiet world without words, a reverie-like state of awareness that would naturally occur in his presence. It feels like a person is very much alive, but also in a quiet, still state of mind. Dr. Marvin told me he had often experienced the big bang's thunderous explosion of sound and light when he was lying on the blue rug. Sounds psychotic. It could be. There is one major difference. He could float in and out of these patterns with some control. He hypothesized that this energy field state is really the home base for all human beings.

DIANETICS: DEALING WITH TRAUMATIC EVENTS

Dr. Marvin and I frequently discussed his views concerning life. He was fully committed to neurokinetic driven energy field expressions, natural self-healing and releasing tensions that had occurred from early traumatic experiences. Dr. Marvin's approach was the L. Ron Hubbard actualization method called Dianetics. Hubbard theorized that there are incidents in your life that have blocked, contracted or limited your human potential. If you can remember these incidents and release the emotional reactions, you will become a clear thinking person. Dianetics uses many of the methods of psychodynamic therapy. Some mental health practitioners accused Dianetic counselors of not having the proper credentials to work with people with these psychic healing methods. Irv, a World War II Army Air Force fighter pilot and one of Hubbard's loyal followers, suggested to Hubbard that they should instead promote Dianetics as a religion. That would end the hassling and they would be eligible for many tax benefits. Dianetics is now called Scientology.

I had studied this Hubbardian approach extensively for a

number of years and even spent many hours being "audited," (undergoing the Dianetic memory recovery and tension releasing therapy). My therapist Blake worked with me for many hours processing incidents that I was recalling about my early life. Our sessions were deep, intensive and very emotional. Our work uncovered a major incident that had plagued me most of my life.

Just after I turned four, an older teenage boy who lived upstairs in my house spazzed and threatened to throw me in the poky (the furnace in the basement) if I told anyone what had happened to us. As an adult, I could not recall what really happened. A very young boy really only has a vague memory of actual traumatic events. Anyway, it was a threat that totally traumatized me. To the adult mind, this appeared to be something sexual in nature and Blake, of course, first hypothesized he had uncovered a sexual trauma because of my resistance and extreme difficulty in processing this situation.

After processing this traumatic event with Dr. Marvin with no resolution, I found it resurfacing during the baseball World Series of 2013. At this time I happened to be coaching Josh, a young minor league baseball pitcher. We were focusing on his breathing patterns and motor movements during his pitching delivery, particularly how he was using his legs and pelvic core. Our interaction reminded me of the joy I provided for my professional teachers at an early phase of my career. Out of nowhere, the old event began to replay in my head. As a young lad I had a wild fondness for opening car doors and attempting to start the old automobiles that were often parked in back yards in my neighborhood. People did not lock their cars in those days and the ignition turned easily to produce a satisfying staccato rumble. Then came the thump and jolt which excited me to no end.

It seems that this mischievous boy (me) had opened the door of Arthur's old black Chevrolet and was in the process of starting it. This car was Arthur's prized possession. From his perspective, I invaded it. This invoked such intense angry threats that they were too much for a young boy to emotionally handle. Youngsters employ the defenses of projection, denial and distortion to ward off anxiety and the memories associated with this kind of experience.

Arthur's sister, Jenifer, heard him yelling at me and came out of the house. She picked me up, hugged and comforted me. She even gave me a lollypop. A horrific event turned sweet. I have had many warm feelings for Jenifer since I recovered the original incident. Needless to say, I still love old cars and would prefer to drive one of these shit boxes. Events like the one I have described are called an attraction to the trauma. That happens because intense emotional events, either pleasant or unpleasant, arouse the clusters of neurons that are adjacent to each other in the brain. I will describe how this happens in chapter eleven.

Dr. Marvin also shared with me an event from his boyhood. He had experienced a strong bodily reaction to the surgical instruments that had been inserted deep in his throat during a tonsillectomy. He continued to feel a frequent gagging reflex and could not satisfactorily resolve his reaction to that event.

Many years later, Blake handed down to me several of Hubbard's personality charts that reflected his interest in labeling a person's emotional capacity to feel and relate. They were referred to as "Tone Scales." The Dianetic approach operates with a powerful hypnotic assertion that a person has encountered a trauma that is impairing their present functioning. In many ways, the Dianetic approaches and techniques are no different from those of some present day trauma psychotherapeutic practices.

CONTROVERSIES IN SEXUAL TRAUMA TREATMENT

Not that many years ago I consulted with Nancy, a woman now in her early forties. She had been raped in her late teens. She was enrolled in a specialized cognitive therapy behavior technique called "exposure" in a women's trauma group psychotherapy program. This highly touted treatment is designed to intensify a patient's symptoms with the expected result that a person will no longer be overwhelmed by their traumatic experiences. The techniques used are very similar to those used in Dianetics. This treatment approach operates on the principle and expectation that if a person is constantly exposed to their traumatic event, their symptoms will recede and they will be healed.

Nancy's rape occurred late one evening more than twenty years ago. She was walking back from work to her quarters on her military base when a man darted out from a cluster of bushes. He grabbed her, placed a cloth over her mouth and dragged her back into the woods and raped her. Nancy felt totally violated, stunned and shocked by what had happened. She wanted to tell someone, but kept it to herself. She felt she would be made fun of and punished. Her female bosses were productivity-oriented and demanding. She eventually shared what happened with a friend who advised her to keep it quiet.

After finishing her tour in the military, Nancy married and had children who are now adults and living on their own. Her marriage lasted less than seven years. "I was cold and numb from the rape. I never told him or anyone. I just could not express loving feelings. So he left. I have had so many men. They all do the same. They tell me I am beautiful, but cold, and drop me. I want to be able to have a warm and loving relationship."

Nancy was active in her job as an X-ray technician and taught a course in a junior college. She loved to ride motorcycles and was attracted to martial arts and yoga. She expected that the trauma exposure treatment would improve the quality of her life. Instead, the emotionally arousing and flooding techniques produced constant intense headaches, irritability, sleep problems, lack of energy and low self-esteem. The anxious, panicky feelings that she experienced after she was raped began to constantly reoccur.

"I can't tell the women in the group how I am feeling. The therapists are just like the bosses I had in the military. They are always putting pressure, intimidating and trying to make me do something to please them. They really don't care how I feel. I have nothing in common with them and the other women in the group. My lifestyle and issues are different. I just want a loving relationship with a man and look what I got myself into."

Unfortunately, the majority of therapists that conduct these exposure-based treatment groups are very goal focused and have limited training in psychodynamic group therapy. They often lack the skills to process their patients' anger, confusion and emotional resistance. It appeared that in Nancy's group there was little processing or comforting around the deep emotional issues being activated.

I felt Nancy's pain and chose to empower her to become an active collaborator in her treatment instead of responding as a passive victim. I told her that she had a choice to stay or leave the group and encouraged her to talk with the leaders about our meeting and her reactions to what was happening. We discussed a previous session where she shared with me her interest in martial arts and yoga and how satisfying they were for her. She was now staying at home by herself in the evening and I suggested that she enroll in a yoga class to try to relax and cope with her loneliness.

I have treated several women with sexual trauma issues that were helped by practicing yoga. One of my patients, Kendra, shared with me symptoms similar to Nancy's. She also experienced sexual trauma with severe reactions. After several months of intense emotional flooding from her exposure treatment in her women's trauma group, Kendra began to feel so devastated that she began drinking and even cutting herself to numb her pain. At my suggestion, Kendra enrolled in yoga classes. These sessions provided a major social network for meeting and engaging with people in a more natural and calming environment. As Kendra became more involved in yoga and other recreational pursuits, her symptoms began to subside and recede. She was much more interested in her life in the present and her future. She eventually came to view her trauma as something that happened in the past. Another patient, Sandra, had also been raped. She chose a women's yoga class instead of a trauma group as a tool to help her heal from the sexual violations she had experienced. Sandra eventually developed a strong sense of self and was very active in helping other rape victims recover. She became the CEO of a successful business.

It is interesting to note that my suggestion about doing yoga was upsetting and considered non-scientific by Nancy's treatment team. They had little background in the psychodynamic group processes that were occurring in their cognitive, evidence-based exposure treatment protocols. Hubbard's Dianetic trauma releasing methods were ineffective and disappointing for many people. The calming effects of yoga are now being used in the Overcoming Adversity and Stress Injury Support (OASIS) Project directed by Dr. Paul Sargent and his colleagues at the Naval Medical Center in San Diego. We need to seriously evaluate the treatments we are offering to women like Nancy who ask for help. Theirs is a simple request to alleviate the pain of trauma and look to the future. As Nancy said, "I so want to meet someone, relate, feel love and be happy."

MEETINGS WITH SPENCER

My therapeutic approach to helping people is to release the pent up bodily tensions in my patients through elevating their energy patterns. Drs. David Kupfer and Fritz Perls had skillfully taught me that there is always some resentment that has to be expressed that releases the tension associated with traumatic experiences.

Before we understood what PTSD was really about,
Jonathan, one of my psychology interns, was treating
Spencer, a returning marine from Vietnam. They requested a
consultation session because they felt they were at an impasse
and little therapeutic value was taking place in their sessions.
Within minutes of our three-way meeting, Spencer had very
uncomplimentary things to say. He "God damned" me and
called me an asshole and other insults. His rage was intense.
My student was in shock. He had never experienced his patient
having such an intensely furious energetic reaction. I had
been to the office earlier in the day, so was very calm, centered
and in a highly neutral frame of mind. I had witnessed Fritz
Perls generating the same type of experiences in his Gestalt
psychotherapy workshops.

Spencer wondered why he experienced such a negative
reaction. Our session was about twenty minutes, after which
time Jonathan and Spencer resumed their session. He felt I was
making fun of him during our consultation. I told Jonathan
to encourage Spencer to express his resentment towards me,
which he did for many months. Eventually he began to disclose
his recreational substance use while in Vietnam. Jonathan was
furious when Spencer told him this, because he had asked him
these questions earlier and Spencer had denied using these
substances. I had to process Jonathan's own rage reaction to
Spencer and explain that events are often buried in deeper
recesses of the mind and it is only through connecting to the
emotions that events can eventually surface, be dialogued and
tensions released.

After two years, Jonathan was in the process of terminating
his training at our facility and was working on future treatment
plans for Spencer. To our amazement, Spencer requested that I
become his therapist.

Our initial meetings were cordial. I felt this would not last.
Whenever someone spazzes at you, as Spencer initially did with

me, there is a story to be told. We laughed at the anger and rage he felt toward me at first in that meeting with Jonathan, his former therapist. We established good contact and began talking about his marriage, young son and the issues going on in his life. Still, I instinctively knew that there was something else he wanted to discuss with me.

On an early Thursday evening, we were sitting quietly in my office. There were always long periods of silence during our meetings, but I sensed Spencer wanted to tell me something. Spencer was breathing, sighing and struggling to speak. He previously had had panic attacks that resulted in him being rushed to the emergency room for potential coronary issues. The prolonged silence continued. I felt if he left the session without expressing himself he would be more upset. With some gentle prodding on my part, he softly whispered his story as he began talking about a battle scene.

"It's so hard for me to tell you." He stopped speaking as he gasped for air and sat silently for many minutes. Then he continued, "I was the lead gunner."

All of a sudden Spencer became frozen, totally still. His face became ashen as he took on a lifeless posture. Spencer could not speak. Several minutes of eerie silence followed. Our eyes became wide and locked in as we both held our breath in horror. After what seemed like an eternity I whispered, "Your gun would not fire."

Softly, sadly, he whispered back, "How did you know that?"

He then began sobbing out how so many of his fellow marines had been killed.

"If only I used my own rifle instead of the company one, things would have been different; so many of my fellow marines were killed. I was shot in the chest. I feel so ashamed and cowardly. I should have died too. Why am I here talking with you? It is all my fault. I still feel so responsible."

We continued to sit still as the horrible sounds of battle and unspeakable panic reverberated in his consciousness and flowed into me. There was nothing for me to say. Just a gulp of my breath from sharing the sudden shock of the horrors of battle that never really goes away.

"Why am I here talking with you?" He was furious at me. I knew this was good because he would not turn on himself like so many others who try to kill themselves.

"It is all my fault. I still feel so responsible. You know my secret. You know me too much. I never want to see you again." I felt the wild anger, rage and violation that Spencer was feeling being transferred right into me.

Survivor's guilt is hell. "What can I say?" I thought to myself. I told Spencer I would be there for him whenever he wanted me. I knew that he was beginning to consciously own what had happened in battle. He had expressed himself and released some of the negative energy of his trauma.

I felt compassion for Spencer and knew that I could not provide him the physical comfort he so needed, but that Karen his wife could. She was very loving, and actively involved in his treatment. They had known each other since high school days and married upon Spencer's return from Vietnam. I knew he would share with her his reaction that had taken place in our therapy session.

In about a year's time, Karen and he had another child. He asked her to telephone me to ask my opinion, because he told her I knew him the best and he was thinking of having a vasectomy. We chatted pleasantly, but I begged off on that one and suggested to her that he should arrange to see a new therapist to discuss this matter.

As a side note, Spencer then continued his treatment with Sarah Haley, one of the pioneer clinicians who had conceptualized and originated the diagnosis of PTSD. He continued to wail about me with her for several months. I would check in with her from time to time. Sarah knew me well since we grew up in the same neighborhood, attended the same school and had many family connections.

The energy that Spencer and I shared over forty years ago never goes away. Instead, there is a soft melting and fading that flows into a mysterious cloud of seeking redemption and forgiveness. I was on Spencer's dark shadow side that Carl Jung so neatly described.

In contrast, I had played the comforting role in Frankie's treatment, whereas Owen, his cousin whom Frankie loved and adored and turned on, was the receptacle of his anger, rage and projections. Owen had done so much psychically and materially for Frankie, yet Frankie projected his negative dark side onto him. I wish I could have told Frankie to show more love and gratitude for him and less for me. It doesn't work that way. The shadow sits silently and has its own mysterious manner of expression.

ZACK, SEARCHING FOR LOVE: A YOUNG PHYSICALLY AND PSYCHICALLY WOUNDED WARRIOR

Over the years I have come to realize that therapists need to tolerate the vituperative spazzes that are emitted as tension is being released. Projecting a problem or situation onto another person is a key component of this healing process. If the patient can eventually become aware of their projecting the dark side of their psyche onto another person, there is major growth. If not, they become stuck in a paranoid, defensive mode of relating to the world. The late president, Richard Nixon, was purported to state: "Just because you are paranoid, does not mean they are not out to get you."

During the Vietnam War clinicians were attempting to understand and help veterans who were returning from battle. Their perspectives and approaches varied. Some veterans healed and moved on, others were stuck in the terror of their experiences. Rage reactions, self-destructive behavior and substance misuse did not fit into the rational, verbal approaches that were the standards of practice. What is known is a major factor in successful therapeutic outcomes is whether there is a significant other in a person's life. When there is no other, the therapist has to fill in the gap until he or she is dismissed.

Such was the situation with Zacharias. He had been wounded in Vietnam. It seems he threw a grenade in battle that bounced off enemy forces, but somehow returned and wounded him in the chest. After he was discharged from the Army, he spent the next year just staying around his parent's house and spending a lot of time in bed. I was the only outreach worker in the area who was active in dealing with returning Vietnam vets. All my colleagues were working with WWII or Korean vets. There were major age and cultural differences. I was even screamed at by the reception clerk when I walked into another VA hospital. I was there to give a talk to the staff on these very issues and differences. I was the go-to psychologist to meet with these guys. The politicians were demanding action. I was ordered to do something. There was no plan, just an attempt to find a solution to the returning veterans' difficulties. This is not how things are done today. Shunning veterans and calling them names to their faces like "baby killer," was not uncommon.

Trying to get Zack to the clinic was a chore. He did not show up for his appointment on the first few attempts, but with some prodding and caring, we finally met. He was six feet tall with reddish blond hair, a golden boy. Zack did not view himself as troubled. He had been a very good athlete, acted extremely friendly and often would tell me to "listen up" when he was making a point about something. Our connection was dynamic. He talked a lot about the sweats he was experiencing and his difficulty in socializing. I presented my work with Zack in our clinic seminars. Mixed anxiety and depression was the working diagnosis. Zack and I talked about going back to college. He had been drafted while he was studying for a business degree. After about six weeks, Zack spazzed at me as his once joyful asshole veneer turned into a rage, "You just talk. You are a NATO clinic" (No Action Talk Only). His turning on me was not unexpected.

I would call him on the phone, but could not make contact. I did not see him for nearly two years. He just stayed at home with his parents and his younger siblings. The Massachusetts congressman, a family friend who lived in his neighborhood, telephoned again to our administrators, "We are so disappointed you cannot do more for this veteran."

In the 1970s we were trying everything to help our young Vietnam vets. They did not view themselves as having a psychiatric diagnosis. In fact, they ran their own self-help groups. It was like I was back in the navy again. There was a close camaraderie between us. They knew I had been a navy medic. All this boundary stuff did not exist. I knew no more than they—just a good listener who took verbal punches on the chin. We had an outreach program for individuals who would not come into our clinic. I would meet these vets at a gym, bar, or park. We would talk and go for walks.

I finally persuaded Zack to go for a walk. Soon we started to work out and swim together. The huge abdominal scar from his wound was slowly healing. We talked about his wish to date and return to his old social self. I just listened. He did most of the talking. I was, in a sense, his shadow other self.

After a few weeks he became very excited. His low level of energy elevated to a highly excitable state. My secretary blandly took a telephone message for me that Jesus Christ had called. He planned to die at three o'clock the next day, which was Friday. He was obviously delusional and his mood had changed from one of withdrawal and depression, to elation and excitement. His mother also called to inform me that Zack had become very religious. I was already committed for that Friday afternoon and did not want to participate in his delusional drama of dying and returning to life again. I told him I could see him on a Sunday afternoon.

Friday passed and on Sunday he announced that his new name was Zacharias, after the biblical Zacharias. He was like an oracle in his resurrected state of happiness and well-being. In his highly grandiose and extremely verbal state, he announced that he was talking with women and soon would be making love again. He was proud to inform me that he had emptied the shower room at the gym as he related the following tale. Guys were showering, perhaps six or so, and were discussing how they would like to beat up on a group of people. He joined in on the conversation and said to them, "Have you ever killed anyone?" A shrugged headshake, "No!" From Zack, "I have, and I have scars to prove it."

A shocked silence descended. The men abruptly cleared the shower, dressed, and ran from the gym. Zack happily continued his ablutions and walked out calmly. As he reported this incident an eerie silence enveloped my office. We continued to talk. He tearfully expressed to me that he felt so ashamed that he had killed women and children while he was in battle. I knew that was enough and we ended our session. He asked me to hug him. There was the close embrace of brothers consoling one another during a horrific tragedy. We parted. I knew something was going to change.

In a few weeks, we had another session at which time Zack's emotional state had totally altered from elation to sadness, sullenness, and an angry sulkiness. I knew I was about to get it, and out it came. "You are a cheater, a liar, a cocksucker, and a cunt. You are no fucking good. I know there's some sexual connection between us and you are up to something. You suck." After releasing his tension, Zack put me on a sabbatical for over a year. I will explain Zack's pseudo-sexual projections in chapter eleven.

He sought me out again, "I got to get back with you."

He wanted to be my friend. At the same time I was his worst enemy. "What can I do with him now?" I wondered to myself. Remember, there were no standards for practice in those days. Be effective, be creative was the expectation and norm.

After we reconciled, I brought him to Dr. Marvin at the office. "Let them share him," I thought. He loved it for about six months. He fit in well with the group. The silence and stillness helped heal the intense explosions of battle that were lingering in his consciousness. His reflections about what was transpiring had also helped me observe what was happening in my own life.

Dr. M's talk of living in a cave was too primal for someone who had suffered the horrendous military fright of battle. Zack angrily spat out his opinion of Dr. Marvin and his group. "They are worse than me. They hang here and talk of some distant future living in a cave. They wouldn't know how to wipe their ass if it came to that. I've seen all that shit. They are just another NATO group (no action talk only). Reminds me of all the Jews in the desert waiting to go to the Promised Land. Hope it happens in my lifetime." He left.

A year later we met a few times at the gym. Time was passing. Five years had elapsed since we first met. Zack felt he was going nowhere. He moved out of his family home and lived in a first floor apartment in town by himself. He enrolled in a few college classes but never finished. When I was in his neighborhood, I'd bang on his window and say hello. He loved it and hated me for my interest. He returned to his silence. A few more years had passed when he called to let me know that something nice was happening in his life. He was living with a woman named Eleanor and her two children. Zack and I began a series of sessions in my office. I coached him on some social amenities. He even obtained a job, which provided him a structure around which he built his life. Eleanor conceived and a beautiful daughter became the love of his life. When I met him from time to time, an infectious smile would come over his face. He felt love and connection; he felt healed. He needed me no more. There was a warm embrace, a laugh and a little talk. Our work had been completed.

CHECKING OUT AND MOVING ON

Several years later I began to drift away from intense involvement at Dr. Marvin's office after unexpectedly stumbling into my next encounter, an adventure with an Indian meditation teacher that I called "Himself." I still maintained my cordial contact with Dr. Marvin until he died in 2008. Things were changing for me. Our family was blessed with another daughter and son. Many professional commitments drew my attention. The group seemed stuck. All that talk of disaster and living in caves was just a delusional manifestation of a dark energy pattern from my point of view.

6.

WESTERN JOURNEY TO THE EAST

THE LIBERATED ONE

One gloomy Saturday afternoon in November, as black clouds ominously signaled the beginnings of heavy rain, I moved indoors, trading my usual activity of raking leaves for a paintbrush. As I stroked on the paint, my mind began matching the rhythm of my arm rising and falling with snippets of conversations I had the previous week with a number of my colleagues about a transpersonal psychology conference taking place later in the afternoon. Family life was good. We were expecting a new arrival in the early summer.

I found myself changing gears and arriving at the conference twenty minutes before the event was scheduled to begin. There was an overflow crowd of maybe 2,000 participants. The conference organizers had everyone seated in an orderly fashion. Everything was tranquil, no pushing, no rushing. It was exciting for me to say hello to old colleagues and friends. This Indian sage, Himself, was to be the featured speaker. A tranquil choral sound filled the air. There were a few introductory speeches and soon thereafter Himself arrived. He sat on a handcrafted, oversized, orange-draped, cushioned chair and soon began laughingly relating to the audience as he began to speak in his native Indian dialect. A young lady, clad in a pleasant dress and well-coiffured hair, provided a translation in English every few minutes. The title of his talk was "The Psychology of the Mind." He told story after story, mostly mythology, not really anything about himself or his life experiences. Eventually, he came around to making his point that the control center of the mind was the heart. I began to observe myself becoming agitated and soon began thinking that this man was some sort of an illogical maniac who knew no brain science or any of the psychology that I had studied. After listening to him rave to the audience for a forty-minute, mind-torturing experience, I had had enough. I got out of my seat and wanted to leave. Instead of walking out, I worked my way from the side to get a closer view of this wild man and his chicanery. There was something else happening, but it did not have much to do with what he was saying. He was so content with himself. The smile on his face, teasing with the joyful and fun-making expression of a young child, melted my technique-oriented, critical mind and replaced it with a curiosity to find out what was happening here. It certainly was not the psychology that I had learned to practice.

Later in the evening, I returned to my painting project in the basement. His bold contention that the area around the heart was the control center of the mind was too much to take. My view of the world was being challenged at many levels. What does he know? Had he ever read any brain research in English? Most likely not.

I dropped in to see Dr. Marvin early the next week. I was rather serious in my description of what had transpired. Dr. Marvin seemed to be amused by what I had told him. He knew quite a bit about Himself, but did not want to say anything about what I was experiencing. He thought it would be better if I could figure things out for myself. "Maybe we could show these people a thing or two about trance states and breathing patterns," I thought.

I began to experience another energy grabbing me and sparking my curiosity to check out what this guy was about. The sound of his voice reverberating through my mind was enough to draw me to experience his two-day program. When I arrived at a spacious auditorium in the middle of Boston's major medical area, I found 300 people sitting comfortably on cushions on the floor, a few were sitting on chairs. Since I was the last to arrive, I spotted an area in the back where I could sit on either the floor or a chair. I carried my notepad with me. This was supposed to be a seminar I thought. I scanned around the room as my attention was drawn to a group of young men and women with shaven heads and orange robes sitting in front of a plush, large, orange-covered chair. A few baskets of flowers were tastefully placed on each side. There was a quiet excitement as Himself, in a powerful, gentle fashion, paraded down the aisle and eventually planted himself in a comfortable lotus posture on his chair. All this time the audience was chanting a soothing, repetitive, hypnotic sound.

Himself eventually began to speak about the psychology of the mind. He presented his theoretical approach to the origin of the universe in terms of the big bang theory and the origin of matter as being generated from vibrant contractions of light and sound. I started to take a few notes but soon stopped, as I was lulled out of my conscious mind into a trance. A comforting presence pushed me into some kind of reverie. I did not know what to do. I just sat still. I talked to nobody, really knew nobody, but felt OK.

People could go up and greet this teacher after his talk. I did not bother. I made some notes as I tried to remember what he had been talking about, but it did not seem to matter. I had been transposed into a peaceful stillness in which there are no words, just inner quiet. Soon thereafter a coffee break was scheduled. A few sips of the java tasted like nectar. I felt calm and tranquil with nothing to say to anyone. We soon would be sitting on the floor again. This guru guy was going to touch you as you sat quietly with your eyes closed.

I certainly knew how to sit quietly. I had done it with Dr. Marvin. Himself came cruising by in the total darkness. He touched my head. I reacted with a slight growl. Then a contemplative peacefulness overcame me as I watched my breath flow in and out while a subtle blue dot was floating in front of my closed eyes.

After this meditative session we all filed out to an area where we were treated to a wonderful vegetarian luncheon as I suddenly became aware of how hungry all these new events had made me. In the afternoon, there was another talk and again a visit from Himself. This time when he touched me I let out a wild growl. This had happened before at the office with Dr. Marvin, but not with the same intensity.

I felt good, went home to my family. There were three words to remember, I could not memorize them. I had been mesmerized by the sounds that were vibrating throughout my entire body and mind. I threw away my notes. "This is deep hypnotic trance stuff," I said to myself.

Sunday was pretty much the same. The blue dots were floating, the sound was vibrating, I was laughing, full of love. There was plenty of rage under that love. What I became aware of is that the "ME" is just a small part of a higher energy that encourages creativity and a connection to a universal sound and light that has no language, but a force of love and connectedness. This guru must take a lot of negative energy, I thought. It is a piece of work to handle all these people. I returned home to my family, armed with a few chanting tapes. I began to remember the words we had been chanting. I had heard this sound many years ago, it sounded then like, "I am a wire." The words are secondary to the primal, vibrational sounds that generate a pleasant peacefulness.

I continued in my role as a teacher and therapist. I seemed to be happier. I was suddenly able to rise above my own resentment and the demanding expectations of my superiors. It seemed that Himself's laughter had found its mysterious way inside me, nudging aside that serious mind of mine.

Himself left town early in the week. I dropped by his center. His picture was everywhere. The group was singing a different chant. I thought it was weird, but hung around. Doing a little volunteer physical service was part of the program. I volunteered to vacuum the carpets in the meditation hall. A wild surge of energy came over me. There were picture cards of Himself. An inner voice said, "Take this," and I did. It was neat. I was in a comfort zone state of relaxed awareness and soon returned home happy and excited to share my energetic joy with my family.

I continued visiting the center to chant and meditate. I was a bit of a problem in that these ungodly sounds would flow out of me. They are called *kriya* sounds, just like a lion roaring. They felt so damn good, but they scared other people around me. Himself had written in his autobiography about his experiences of these roaring sounds. It is conjectured that this is energy flowing from lower to higher centers. Modulating and neutralizing negative energy is the result of this experience.

During the winter I had an opportunity to meet with other meditation masters. I did think Himself activated a horrific rage in me. It was the same rage that I had been experiencing with my combat Vietnam patients who had been expressing their reaction to what they had been through. They were swearing and cursing me, lots of sexual projections and expletives. I, however, was just growling.

Himself never paid any attention to me, or really, any other male. He was totally involved in himself and what was interesting to him. My mind concocted an image of him as a dog that was always sniffing someone or something, especially the young attractive women in his presence. His only major complaint was the uncomfortable sensations he experienced from the perfume the women had been using. What I did experience was my energy transacting with his energy. It certainly was not a rationally programmed technique. It was like interacting with the ancient oracles of Greece and Rome as my old emotional and reptilian brain was being activated and refined. Unwanted tensions were releasing. Soon a powerful, all encompassing love began to surge into my awareness. "Learn to eat your anger," I was told by other inner psychic science practitioners with whom I consulted about my classical love/hate relationship with Himself. People loved to obey him and focus on his every word. I laughed a lot at what he had to say, but something was happening that was good.

Now this guy was an authentic soul of souls. He talked a lot about his own teacher and his constant connection with his teacher's energy and presence. Huge photographs of his teacher were on display everywhere. I found myself more attracted to these images than looking at Himself in person. They pierced right through my very being, coming alive in my awareness as the real energy of a living human being. It was like this teacher was transacting with me, rather than Himself. This heart-thumping, contenting experience was nice, believable, and transforming. The young boy in me could sense the hero connection. Many of the other males had the same take on Himself. Every young lad has a sports hero. This simple, dark-skinned handsome teacher of Himself referred to as *Nitya* (always happy), offered the image so described by seekers throughout the ages, that is, someone who never took on the cares, joys, and sorrows of a carnal life, but lived simply in detachment. Now Himself was nothing like this simple, silent, Nitya. He loved money, art, and women, at the same time he provided drama, excitement and lifestyle transformation to his fans throughout the world. Some individuals could not deal with his secret, personal lifestyle that had nothing to do with what he was providing his students. Suffice it to say, people came from all over the world to spend time with him.

They would assemble in a long line, and be greeted by him as he sat with a translator and an inner circle sitting around him. People would ask a question. They would get a response similar to the oracles of old. They would feel full of good will as they returned to their seat in the hall. Now there really was not much to say in these transactions. He was referred to as a god man, all knowing, emotionally powerful. Everyone got something. There always was that inner disappointment that he was not listening to ME. But there was another compelling, attractive and inviting energy field present. That verbal talk really did not matter. The inner joy was more rewarding, the feeling of being good and full, was the experience people were seeking and received.

One other note. Himself stated that the human body is like a piece of fruit. As people would approach him, they would bring fruit as a gift. It would be gathered and prepared as a delicious fruit cup that was served for lunch the following day. People ate very well at his place, good vegetarian soup, salad, and other mixes, plenty of it. Participants at the center were expected to help, cook, clean, and maintain. There was a good feeling in these experiences, though you could be pushed to fatigue at times.

Things dramatically came to an end when our hero leader suddenly left the world with a heart attack. I was crushed and deeply saddened. This guy whom I loved and hated, who really didn't give a hoot about me, who would see me and ignore me, had croaked. My young son and he liked each other. Something more than sharing the same birthday was deep between them. This blue-eyed boy at the age of five could sit motionless for two hours with this man. Himself would give him a piece of candy, which my son called a suck, and made him joyful and contented. He was very much moved and he mourned his loss, which he soon forgot. His sister, who was three years older, loved to laugh and play with the other young girls and eat the delicious food.

Good fortune fell upon me as a wonderfully engaging, young breath master, Indiana Blue Eyes, had taken up residence in a nearby town. He had also been a student of Himself and had developed a following of his own. This engaging energy master, who had experienced and trained in many cultural approaches to refining and elevating energy patterns, related to people personally in a joyous, loving and caring fashion. One thing was for sure, he could put energy into you, much in the same way as Himself.

Nice things were happening during these times as I learned to stay centered, keep my energy in a positive upward flow, and provide for my family. The tools I used were a compilation of breathing, chanting, gym work, aerobics, and swimming. I was trying to make sense of what I was doing professionally and personally. How does the love sickness that I was being taught by Drs. Semrad and Arsenian fit into the psychology of the mind proposed by Himself? How could my patients' blocked energy patterns and emotional scars from love-related problems be effectively treated? How did Himself's energy patterns of tranquility, well-being, peace and happiness, fit into the nature of trance-like or hypnotic states?

UNDERSTANDING OUR FLOWING ENERGY FIELDS

My professional, academic interest continues to be exploring the positive and negative effects of the hormones and neurotransmitters generated from our archaic brute-brain that Himself had activated in many others and me. They have to be acknowledged and elevated to the higher, frontal brain in order to effectively relate and communicate. As you recall, I referred to this surging base-brain energy pattern when I discussed the love-sick Lars and the excitement, anxiety and consequences of his behavior. It frequently surges in each and every one of us and can induce us into behaving like an asshole (chaotic, emotional brain energy patterns).

This mysterious flow is the creative, driving force in our relating and searching in matters of love. I believe that it is the basis of trance and altered states of consciousness that often can overtake and overwhelm us. This mysterious energy pattern surfaced during Alexander the Great's chance encounter with a renowned Indian yogi who was living in a forest. This yogi lived simply off the land and, it was rumored, wore no clothes. He rarely spoke, but people were drawn to his serene presence and psychic energy. Alexander was struck with curiosity and excitement and longed to meet with this unusual holy man. Reputed to be godlike, Alexander possessed the disposition and physique of a fierce warrior. On the other hand, he had been educated by Aristotle in the many expressions and complexities involved in matters of love. He dispatched one of his lieutenants to summon this yogi to his quarters so that he could find out what he was about. The sage was not in the least impressed and did not budge. Even when threatened with death if he did not comply, the yogi replied that someone could destroy his body but not his connection to the life force energy that cannot be destroyed, just recycled.

When the lieutenant relayed the yogi's response to Alexander, his excitement grew and he felt even more compelled to meet the yogi and took off to the forest to further pursue this quest. Following his dramatic meetings with this psychic sage, Alexander became tortured by an intense surge of inner, psychic love as he yearned for emotional satisfaction and fulfillment. His tensions were released as powerful sensations vibrated throughout his entire body. He experienced the sensually arousing, pleasurable, as well as the heart-wrenching sensations, that mystics of all religions have described.

THE PSYCHIC CENTERS

What is this psychic energy that the yogi, and my teacher, Himself, transmitted? It is an intense, elevated energy pattern that begins from a mysterious psychic plane, flows through our physical bodies and manifests itself through our breathing patterns, bodily movements and expressions. As it moves, it vibrates throughout our physical body and can be trained to flow from the sitting bones located in our pelvic floor, upwards to the top of our head. Inner psychic practitioners have charted this circular or winding, subtle energy system which, when activated, flows inside each of us through seven major body centers. Our goal is to bring up the energy that is generated near the buttocks and base of the spine (the sacral plexus) through our psychic centers, each having its own unique energy and vibration, to the top of the head.

This is not something for the dabbler to engage in. It requires commitment and discipline on the part of the practitioner. In this process one becomes aware of happy states, as well as the all-pervasive, irrational madness of love described by Plato and many philosophers. It is an experience in which we become connected to everyone and everything. In this deep, psychic, state we feel very godlike and full of love. We see our reflection in people's faces, in mountains and rivers, in life's simple joys and sorrows. There is a oneness to everything and everybody. Manifestations of different colors are often common to this experience. All our neurotransmitters and hormones can be activated in this process. The whole world feels interconnected. This is a trance or hypnotic pattern that I will describe in chapter nine.

Accessing and connecting to these energy patterns all begins with working towards an awareness of our seven major psychic centers. Center one is our root center, located in the sitting bones beneath our pelvic floor. It is referred to as the sacral plexus and is sometimes referred to as the "holy bone." The self-centered, beauty-seeking aspect of our personality originates here. This energy center is related to our evolutionary old brain. Highly self-involved beings act as though the sun shines right out of their ass. We humans often fail to recognize that our quest in displaying and seeking beauty needs to be elevated throughout our other psychic centers in order for our creative energy to be activated to transform our awareness.

We refer to others, or even ourselves occasionally, as being a "pain in the ass," or even worse, "an asshole." These colloquial expressions can be more descriptive and accurate than intellectual, scientific expressions. When our psychic energy stays stuck in this root center we become uncomfortable and agitated without knowing why. This joyful, and sometimes painful, center can concern most of us more than we are willing to acknowledge. It is the core of our very private psychic life, particularly in matters of love.

The second center has been described at length by Freud and discussed by me in the chapter on navy days. Yes, it is the sex center. Our limbic emotional brain heavily influences it. When our hormones are activated, consciousness is altered and the entire world is experienced in a sexual manner. Love and all its madness flow from the juices being transmitted from this center. If one can master the flow of this energy and contain the surging hormones, a special magic takes place as it begins to flow upward to a higher plane.

The third power point, called the will center, is located at the level of the navel and relates to one's wants or desires. It has been described as "fire in the belly" or the "belly brain." In more vernacular language it is sometimes referred to as a "gut feeling." This energy is turbulent, fiery and self-seeking. Gastric sensations, stomach tension, "butterflies in the stomach," flight or fight anxiety states originate from this control center.

These three centers are our biological, personal manifestation of our neurokinetic core energy patterns. Do you swagger? Are you called a tight ass? How do you handle your sexual fluids and the expelling of the piss and shit flowing in this area? We usually prefer to use more abstract nouns such as urination and anal defecation when we discuss these topics since we do not want to experience the olfaction involved. The fourth body point, the heart center, is located in the chest and the heart area. It is at this center that we access our vital force energy. It makes no rational sense until you can actually experience this for yourself. You watch your breath as it floats in and out and out and in. When this center is activated, consciousness alters as you float into a creative, blissful state. In the expansiveness of this infinitesimal moment that can feel so long, strong and all-encompassing, you sense you are everywhere. It could be said that this is the center described by Aristotle when he proposed the heart center as the locus of the mind.

When we gently swallow the moisture in our mouth and breathe into our throat, we activate and energize this fifth center flowing down the front of our body through our heart area, navel, and sexual centers to the sitting bones in our pelvis, where it then winds, wiggles and meanders its way up through the neurons in our spinal column to the top of our head. In this state we can drift into a world without words as language is dissolved and our consciousness is enveloped in a unique stillness. When we emerge from this trance state we often discover to our amazement an ability to find words previously unavailable to our awareness that express our positive and negative feelings to the persons we love.

The sixth, or master center, is located between the eyebrows, just above our palate. It is sometimes referred to as the third eye. The oneness of everything is generated through this power spot. Therapists and hypnotists activate their client's restorative energy patterns when they direct them to take in a deep breath as they roll up their eyes, and focus on what they want to see happen. When we are attending to this center, we learn to divert our attention from situations and matters that can arouse anxiety. This center vibrates and promotes a peaceful and somewhat detached perspective of what our life means to us.

Center seven, the still point, is located at the top of the head. When we are accessing the energy field activated in this center, we are connected in mind and body. There is a refined awareness in our participation and transactions with the world as we simultaneously watch and engage in the multifaceted drama of our lives. This is the omnipresent state of love on its highest plane.

HIMSELF'S SECRET HERO: LOVE AND PSYCHIC GYMNASTICS

Late in his life, Himself began to share with his students his role model who dwelled high in the mountains of India about a thousand years ago. This exotic teacher, whom I fondly refer to as Guppy, taught that all you need to experience this vital energy field is a burning desire to want it to happen.

One of the secrets in this lovemaking exercise is for the male not to ejaculate. Ejaculating brings on a death experience, emptiness and a feeling of loss and separation. The old Latin proverb *"Post coitum, triste omni est."* After intercourse, a sad feeling ensues conveys a similar axiom. So too, Dr. Peter Kramer in his book *Against Depression* quotes Aristotle's scientific treatise, *The Problems*: "Why do young men when they first begin to have sexual intercourse, hate those with whom they have associated after the act is over?" Mastering the sexual drive and orgasm requires attention, concentration and containment. When we acquire this skill we become connected to the powerful divine plane of oneness with the cosmos.

Guppy was not like Plato who recommended sexual abstinence, a rising above carnal desire when it came to physically connecting with another individual. Guppy's art form and interaction style were to relate both sexually and psychically, depending on his mood and his biological and carnal needs. Thus, he was simultaneously a hellion and a saint. He acted in a special dual manner. In his mind there was no such thing as good or evil, just breath and sexuality manifesting as beauty and love.

Guppy was known for being both a great spiritual master

and an accomplished lover. He was able to achieve such great control over his mind that he could move in and out of physical, worldly experiences. He was reputed to be someone who could be engaged in sexual activity with his physical body and at the same time be in a totally detached psychic state. Wherever his energy took him to behold beauty, there he would go in a physical, psychic and spiritual manner. This behavior would include a sexual component. In public, Guppy would appear serenely holy, but in private, he loved his wine and enjoyed his sexual practices, that is, sometimes. He could also spend long periods of time in a totally selfless state praying, fasting, chanting and caring for the poor. Pursuing the love searching impulse was only a minor aspect of Guppy's life. It was, however, the source of his creative energy that inspired him to be an artist, musician, writer and poet. During his transmissions and interactions with his followers he was able to transmit a psychic energy that would create joy, happiness and contentment. He was considered to be godlike, a dispenser and transmitter of life force energy. One look from his gaze would pierce through you as though you were being hypnotized. In my opinion, he possessed a perfect psychic power that was reverberating creative energy throughout his physical body.

It was said that when Guppy was engaging in his tantric sexual activity he would merge in an ecstatic, energetic experience with his lover, so that the fire of their sexual passion and the sun of their love blended their two beings into one liquid melting of their body and spirit. As the excitement of this divine madness was peaking, the ecstasy of their combined melting became ethereal, rising into the atmosphere as they surrendered, merged into this heavenly exhilarating union of being at one with everything.

In many ways, this reminds me of my younger days, visiting the "holy houses" (night clubs) with my navy buddies. We felt the same searching and longing. We laughed with each other over our gawking at the showgirls and teased about our attraction to the mysterious energy generated by their dancing. This energy would ride in our consciousness for days, as we would playfully mimic our experiences and encounters at the holy house. We were searching for just what the holy man Guppy was seeking, albeit in a very different manner.

Our human nature drives us to continuously search for this biologically-driven love connection. Some of us are open about it. Others try to deceive one another in covert interactions and do not acknowledge surging energies that are being generated from their archaic reptilian brain. They self-deceive and attempt to fool others with their grandiose assertions that they are beyond searching for love and connection.

The famous British essayist, Samuel Johnson, advised that we should, "Be not too hasty to trust or admire the teachers of virtue. They discourse like angels but they live like men."

What he is asserting is that all human beings are compelled by this vital force to obey her dictates of eating, sleeping and, of course, love-seeking and its expression.

Why would one attempt to explore these methods of relating? These naturally flowing energy patterns enable us to relate to our surroundings and experience love in the ways we want it to work. We acquire skills in mastering the up and down sides of love. I will share my methods for accessing and contacting these elevating energy patterns in chapter thirteen. Our emotional brain transmits its natural smile as we still our minds, and nurture and rejuvenate ourselves with these practices in our quest for love and beauty.

BOOK THREE

PSYCHOLOGICAL PERSPECTIVES ON MATTERS OF LOVE

7.

PRIMARY COMMUNICATION PATTERNS AND ENTITLEMENT

Harrison's Entitlement and Love Searching Adventures

Harrison was not an excitable person like my love-smitten navy buddy, Frolicking Freddie, but rather a rational, reflective and organized attorney who wanted to experience love on his own terms. I must honestly say I thoroughly enjoyed listening to his views on love, particularly his appraisal of a person who did not meet his criteria in his quest for beauty and connection. In that situation, his potential lover would be abruptly dismissed as being Not Good Enough or NGE. Harrison was always upbeat in pursuing his romantic attractions. He even had to carry an appointment book to keep track of his dates. Talk show and television appearances were also part of his repertoire. If matters were not to his liking, he would not hesitate to use the legal system to correct any disappointment and rejection he may have experienced.

This entitled prince would not be considered a handsome figure by most people's standards, only in the adoring eyes of his mother and sisters. He was a heavyset gentleman who wore a bushy hairpiece that set off his round, pug-nosed face and small mustache. His bulging blue eyes were magnified through thick-rimmed glasses. This poor physical presentation did not, however, prevent this very active professional attorney from searching for his ideal mate. He sought out attractive, muscular, beautifully developed bodybuilding women. Embarrassment was not one of the feelings he experienced as he described the arousal that would overtake him as he would gaze at and worship the attractive models exhibiting their voluptuous thighs in female body-building magazines.

This middle-aged Romeo's charm lay in his gift for composing love sonnets to his potential beloved and his enticing, hypnotic, telephone voice. Eventually, he would arrange for a date. On one occasion he made plans to have lunch with Tessie, a body-builder who lived some distance away. He did not like to drive, so was planning to take the bus. I had to restrain myself from providing him honest feedback and a realistic appraisal of his love searching madness. In matters of love, the thinking, rational brain has little influence over the biologically-driven, base brain energies and my advice would not be heeded. It would, in fact, only fuel the madness of Harrison's love searching quest. Harrison sees himself as an entitled, handsome prince who will eventually make love to that perfect charming princess. I meekly requested that he inquire about the return trip schedule at the same time as he was making his preparations. At our next session he angrily inquired about what evidence I had to tell him to plan his return trip and buy a round trip ticket. "What happened?" I inquired.

"She looked at me, scorned me, laughed, and walked away," he said.

"I'm sorry," I said. "Do you think your expectations are too high?"

"No," he said. "It's just a matter of finding the right one."

Harrison is a *godt*, my humorous descriptive label for self-absorbed, self-centered persons who view themselves and act as if they are perfect individuals, entitled to be treated as though they are VIP Hollywood stars with special regal rights and privileges. The psychobiological origin of this flamboyant behavior is related to the natural self-centered, energy-driven display patterns emanating from our archaic reptilian brain.

This evolutionary self-preservative brain stem provides for us the energetic networks for our breathing, eating, rhythm patterns and sexual expression. It sits at the base of the brain that makes life "all about me" at some level. Popular psychology labels this as narcissistic behavior. Dr. Jock Murray, my teacher whose adventures I shared with you in chapter four, was considered an authority on this personality pattern and behavior. He called it narcissistic entitlement. Godts often have little awareness of their social surroundings and tend to express themselves in a very serious, self-involved and entitled manner. It is as though the world is all about ME. After all, love is an infusion of a god-directed energy called *ate*, first described by the Greeks in their mythological tales of the drama, excitement, deception and intrigue engaged in by the gods in their love-seeking adventures.

Godt-like behavior patterns can either amuse or anger individuals interacting with or observing them dramatizing their needs. These outrageous, grandiose attitudes and self-serving expressions can be initially exciting, intriguing and humorous, since we all carry within our reptilian brains similar neurons that are not in our everyday awareness and manner of relating. The downside of these emotional, flooding expressions is that they tend to result in frustration and intense rage, moodiness and disappointment for the godt. Intense ridicule from individuals observing and reacting to their drama can frequently make them withdraw as they sit, sulk and suck something to comfort themselves for the mistreatment they feel they have experienced.

Even though Harrison is unattractive, obese and slovenly, he considers himself entitled to the most beautiful women in the world. There is a tendency for all of us to be godts at certain times. We are all god-like mysterious psychic beings. We dwell, however, in physical bodies and are therefore subject to the rules of the nitrogen and oxygen cycles. As biological beings, our physical needs necessitate that we breathe, reproduce, eat and defecate. At some level we are emotionally driven to parade and share our perfection and delight in ourselves, particularly in matters of love. All of the social media play into this Hollywood godt aspect of our psyche.

Young children are naturally attracted to fairy tales of love, beauty and conflict that reflect this old, reptilian brain, egocentric stage of development. When stress occurs it is natural for them to release the tensions of their disappointments and rejections through intense crying and rage reactions as they often attribute blame to someone or something for the cause of their problem. My metaphor for these emotional, brain tension release outbursts is a spaz. In this manner we are naturally attempting to restore and rebalance our beauty and base brain generated perfection. We like to call this our self-esteem. As Harrison demonstrated, we feel entitled and respond with rage when matters are not to our liking. This brute, snake-like brain state generates within us a totally self-centered and involved absorption. Our inner self-thinking or expressive mantra can be either *Meow, Me Now*, (As self absorbed felines signal, It's all about me) or, if we are being psychically invaded, devalued or angered, we respond with a powerful, melodic, vituperative, emotional brain generated, cursing rage reaction that I call the grand mantra. Remember that "fuck you" thunderous, verbal invasion that would reverberate right through me during my navy days? It says a little something about everything. Energy does not just flow one way. It creates, and also reabsorbs as it recycles itself. That is one of many functions for all of our navy expletives of fuck, shit and piss. Friar Ted once told me that its origin could be traced to the Latin language root *fac* which means, "go make yourself." It calls to our attention that we are not that perfect immortal god who lives on Mount Olympus, but rather a limited, biological being, that must breathe, eat, reproduce and defecate. All primal expressions can also have an opposite meaning. A joyous invocation of the F-sound can be so sweet, arousing and satisfying, as it elevates our emotions to a heavenly state of connection and one with the universe.

While Harrison was spazzing I would often hold my breath in shock and amazement in order to diminish the intensity of the rage reaction that pierced through my physical and psychic system. Even emotionally bland intellectuals can experience some difficulty in ignoring this vituperative psychic bomb. It is sometimes a paradox that we feel separate from the spazzing individual and at the same time are strongly aware of the emotional blast that is taking place. The mad mood of the spazzer screams out loud and cuts right through us at some level, insisting on being acknowledged.

Leopold, nicknamed "suck face", was one of my colleagues who loved to vicariously experience the spazzes of his patients. It was an infusing shock treatment that would wake him up and energize his numbed, lethargic way of relating to the world. A smirking smile, that I would call a "shit eating" grin, would begin to surface on his wrinkled face when someone was angry or spazzing at him. He himself was unable to spaz, so in that moment when someone else was spazzing he could feel alive and human. Emotionally deprived, Leopold had grown up in a strictly academic family where there was a premium on rational thinking. Emotions in Leopold's world were not to be acknowledged, experienced or discussed since there was nothing scientific to be demonstrated or learned. They were a distraction from academic accomplishment. In fact, Leopold's father, intellectually brilliant but emotionally obtuse, took a bottle into his study each evening so he could pee in solitude and not be interrupted by his son. This deprivation of meaningful, emotional contact generated a lifelong deficit that Leopold had to endure. He yearned to experience love and emotional stimulation.

The grand mantra, fuck you, communicates the base-brain's energetic, protective expression being transmitted by someone in this spazzing state. Back in my navy days, my fellow medic, Tilden, would enrich his emotional spazzing expression with the dual invocation of *fuckin' shit*. It would quiver right into our chests, cutting deeply into our startled minds and bodies. Some brain researchers have concluded that both praying and cursing are cousins to this spazzing process and share the same neural brain networks that are located deep within our emotional brain.

As we move on, we are not leaving the mysterious F-sound behind. We cannot seem to express ourselves without it. My patient's stories make that clear.

CONCERNING THRUSH: A CAT'S TUTORIAL ON THE NATURE OF KNOWLEDGE

In order to help Harrison ease the many rejections he had been experiencing in his love searching pursuits, I decided to encourage him to adopt a cat to help him acquire some skills for relating emotionally to someone other than himself and ease the loneliness he was feeling. Finding situations that both the patient and therapist share can usually generate light, meaningful discussions and emotional growth. Our family had just adopted a kitten. Harrison took my advice and did the same. I was hoping that Harrison and I could have some interesting conversations about our cats since at some level cats know more than we do. They have access to more natural, deep-brain, primary energy fields of the world without words.

What a pleasant surprise arrived at our house one early spring morning. She was a charming tiger cat with black and gray stripes painted symmetrically across her dainty body. Shades of gold glistened along her underbelly. My son had been approached by a small, starving kitten, just a few weeks old, roaming the streets of his college town. She presented herself to him so enchantingly that he took her home and even bought her designer high-nutrient cat food and premium sliced turkey to fill out her undernourished frame.

When this small adoptee first arrived at our house at the end of the college term she was very timid, afraid to engage in any interaction. She preferred to be alone and spent much of her time in a cozy corner of the basement. She could be enticed into company only with the offer of food. This kitten's face was beautifully dainty, her posture regal. Timidly, her green eyes would gaze adoringly at us. As she grew and began to explore her world outdoors, she displayed another state, that of a ferocious feline with a fierce countenance and attack stance, ready to pursue any mice and chipmunks who infringed upon her territory.

I felt a great joy and exhilaration as I would watch her lapping water from her special dish with her tiny pink tongue. Frequently she would sneeze after she drank. The sneeze emitted a thunderous turbulence that rushed from her chest and swirled throughout her three-pound frame. That sneeze had a daintiness and a power, that combined contradictorily, to give the feeling of a great being, an oracle perhaps, having spoken, not with words, but with feeling. I named this dainty powerhouse Thrush, since that seemed to be the best word one could find to describe the resonating sound of her sneeze.

It just so happened that the whole experience of Thrush the kitten revived the memory of another female sage called Thrush. She was my boyhood chum's mother. She too, could be a holy terror, a red-haired lady in midlife who was beginning to show signs of wear. There was a quivering and shakiness in her voice as she was frequently heard sneezing loudly in a manner similar to that of this young cat. She was not a person who would edit her thinking or feeling states. What she thought or felt was immediately verbalized. When she spoke, everyone listened. It was like the voice of an oracle or witch one could not ignore. She possessed a nonverbal, trance-like commanding power which, when transposed into words, could carry great weight. As young lads, we mischievous ones were boldly corrected one spring afternoon as we helped ourselves to liquid refreshment from her refrigerator. It may have been some sort of juice. Anyway, she put both of her powerful hands on our heads and with a sharp tug at our hair she dragged at us in her haggard, witchy way with the command, "Drink water." I can still hear her voice and do still drink water. So did Thrush the cat and many others. Her exhortation was prophetic indeed. The experts today tell us all to drink lots of water.

Now Thrush, the kitten, has many stories of her own. She slowly worked her way into the family and learned to enjoy physical contact. She found that she liked to be picked up. She had a wonderful purry motor. Its sound was something special. As one listened, it had a soothing quality. It was even more rewarding when I held her as she purred and offered me a special blessing with licks on my neck and cheek. When she had received as much attention as she needed, she signaled to be let down. To complete this process she emitted a roaring meow to reestablish her control of the situation.

As late spring arrived, Thrush took herself outdoors. She would usually sit on the porch for a few minutes to orient herself to her surroundings. In the warm weather she no longer used her litter box, but recycled her excrement in a special part of the yard, her garden. She interacted with all the insects, birds, chipmunks and other rodents in her territory. She was not too fond of dogs. Within weeks, green grasses grew from the area in which Thrush made her deposits in the soil. She was very proud of her produce as she nibbled blades of grass from her garden. When comfortable and satisfied, she loved moving about the yard, alternating between the shade of her garden's plants and the heat of the sun, depending on her wishes.

Thrush viewed the entire world as being about her. When I was at my busiest, involved in a concentrated task, she would find me and insert herself into the middle of the situation. She would position herself on the computer keyboard in order to direct my attention toward herself. If I was attempting to wrap a package, Thrush would spread herself over the wrapping paper so that she might be a participant in the activity. The other side of this seemingly annoying interference was an adorable, non-intrusive aspect that was quite endearing. Thrush displayed her physical presence, but did not intrude at a psychic level.

I must also point out that Thrush did not communicate solely with her facial expressions and sounds. She frequently signaled and led with her hindquarters. When she desired contact she sat with her rear end facing you. It seems that, to her, her derriere was the most important part of her torso. She loved to be stroked along her haunches. This was Thrush's sacral area. This is a message for us all to observe. This holy, or baseline area, is the psychic center for all living beings. It is in this power spot that psychic energy patterns and expressions originate.

Now this young feline was very savvy. She signaled when she had a need to go outside, be picked up or to eat food. If I had a need she ignored me. She was not interested. There was no reciprocity in this relationship, if one chooses to label it that. She did not listen to me. She had no shame or guilt when she ate my tulips after I told her not to. She looked away, unperturbed at my frustration. Thrush was sweet, loving, engaging, selfish and content with herself. She was a fierce feline who hunted and terrorized mice and chipmunks at one moment and was a dainty kitty a few minutes later that demanded that I cuddle her as she licked my face in rapture. It is sometimes very difficult for us to cope with those fluctuating energy patterns that are so natural for a cat, but are often repulsive and very difficult for us to handle in ourselves.

As for Harrison, he shocked me when he blandly informed me that he dumped his cat, Heidi, because she had been behaving just like Thrush. I was rather startled, and then realized this was how he reacted to women he did not think were good enough. So I playfully teased him, "How can you have a relationship with a human being when you can't even relate to a cat?" He took these comments to heart and acquired considerable insight into his tendency to reject people. During this process he began to mourn Heidi and the loss of her wonderful company.

Thrush was about Thrush. Heidi was about Heidi. They sounded their mantra daily: *"Meow, Me Now."* All of us at times would like to be Thrush or Heidi, no shame or guilt, no responsibility, sit and bake in the sun, totally content, anxiety free, just being, *Me Now.*

SPONTANEOUS, PRIMARY, NONVERBAL COMMUNICATION

Thrush was an excellent communicator in terms of her needs. She could signal when she wanted to go outdoors. She would walk to the door and stand there. If she was not responded to, she recited her mantra *meow.* She also signaled when she wanted to be picked up. If I held her and began another activity, such as reading, she would meow her displeasure and order herself to be put down. When her food dish was empty she sat quietly a short distance away and telegraphed her needs with a nonverbal signal.

This type of communication has been described by St. Augustine and discussed by many philosophers and psychologists. They call this spontaneous or primary communication. In this old brain-directed, primary state of communication, Thrush had little control over what happened. When another cat invaded her garden area there could be hissing and yowling. Did Thrush voluntarily choose to express herself to the other cat? No. Or did the situation demand that she express her emotions? Yes, even if she had a shadowy memory of a previous outcome that was not in her favor. After a period of time this emotional state dissipated and she returned to her normal self. There was nothing symbolic in her transactions. As a very curious feline she was content with her mantra, *"Meow, Me now."*

I, however, as a human being with more advanced brain structures, used secondary communication to observe and analyze Thrush and her many transactional states of play and behavior. In other words, because of my larger frontal brain lobes, I have the capacity to reflect, evaluate and make metaphors about what has transpired, whereas Thrush could not. I frequently came upon her inside the house sitting in a state of regal stillness and composure. She was completely content within herself, in full control and gently endearing. She gazed at me with a serene calmness, inviting me to participate in some mysterious way. She was totally still in this state. I admired her and wished I could be calm like her. That stillness leads me to naturally contact and connect to the life force, to quiet the persistent inner dialogues and cognitions in my mind. Thrush was already there in this primary communication mode.

As I describe these events to you there is an additional dialogue in your head about these situations. You may agree or disagree, or perhaps have more information about cats to express. Our knowledge base increases as we begin to discuss these events. This is secondary communication. Our favorite pastime as human beings is to activate our frontal thinking lobes, cogitate, or "yup" (my metaphor), about what is transpiring at a non-verbal level. We make metaphors about the sensory input and impressions that are transmitting energy from our reptilian and emotional brains and sending signals to our frontal, thinking brain. This provides the information we need to elevate, refine and process these sensory inputs. Sometimes the signals are sound focused, other times visual. They even can be taste, smell, or more often, a mix.

In this mode of processing and evaluating what we choose to communicate to others, we can pose and posture ourselves and even conceal the sensory inputs that are being activated in us. When we are just being literal and using our intellectual mode of thinking, we can deceive ourselves into believing that something is a fact rather than just a metaphor. This can be a common problem for us. Individuals whose thinking style is very analytical and obsessive live in what I call Yupville. They are information oriented and constantly attempting to know the cause of everything. Many of us often believe that we are thinking rationally, but at the same time our old brain's grandiose me that also sits inside our head is fueling and strongly influencing our thought process and behavior.

When we activate our analytical mathematical energy patterns being transmitted by our frontal lateralized brain, we can feel excited and in control. We can, however, be reacting to incomplete and limited information that would totally contradict our conclusions. Our primary oral, anal and phallic modes of communication, that is, pissing, shitting and fucking, still sit very much in our emotional brain, slowly seeking to seep into our awareness as information and situations begin to emotionally arouse and infiltrate our thinking patterns. They are, however, often refined by our value systems and are protected through our mind's mechanisms of defense such as projection and denial. My teachers, Drs. Eric Berne and "Jock" Murray's training therapist, Dr. Paul Federn, described two personality states that can occur simultaneously and influence our behavior. Federn coined the label ego states to describe these often conflicting communication patterns. One relates to what is happening in present reality. The other is reliving or re-experiencing, not just remembering, events that took place during our early formative years. Our primitive old brain's scents, sounds, and impressions are experienced and expressed as though they are happening now.

These crossed communication transactions can be the basis for so much strife and conflict. Our self-serving, emotional brain-driven modes enable us to alter and distort situations to preserve the illusion that it is all about me. Internal thought processes such as, "He's a prick, asshole. She's a cunt, stinker," are often more accurate, primary communicative expressions, but are barbaric and politically incorrect. From a psycho-energetic field perspective, our thinking self contracts and abstracts our sensory sensations and becomes more focused and reality-oriented. It is as though we dampen or ignore the emotional brain's color spectrum and sounds as we think in a flat information-oriented mode of processing and relating. This is rewarding when we are dealing with factual, scientific information, but not so helpful when we are coping with the nonverbal matters of love seeping into our awareness.

These modes of relating have been attributed to a rope-like group of fiber bundles called the corpus callosum that connects the left and right sides of our brain. Our brain's frontal lobes provide us the capacity to lateralize, intellectualize, or yup. Processing information and attributing causes is one of its major functions. Do you ever listen to a love song and become very emotionally moved by the melody? When you later read the words to the song, they can seem so banal and unappealing. Do you wonder why? The melodic sounds are being transmitted from your deep emotional brain. Tolerating contradictions in matters of love can make our life intriguing and mysterious as we cope with the anxiety from conflicting communication signals surging from our emotional brain energy fields. In matters of love, the often-used cliché that, "the right hand does not know what the left hand is doing," is a metaphor for the confusing, and often contradictory, primary and secondary communication signals. The initial surging of the love-seeking, emotionally-driven brain can activate a strong physical, sensual attraction and attachment. The thinking, rational brain has its own set of rules and requirements for emotional and intimate engagements. When these two competing brain states are not synchronized, the relationship fades and fails. Mature human communication requires the skill to operate in an abstract manner and contain the powerful, energetic forces that flow through us. Chapter thirteen introduces us to sensory awareness exercises that activate and enrich our sensory awareness and primary communication skills.

Thrush did not possess the large frontal cortex of humans to engage in the secondary communication process, so she did not have to deal with these confusing messages. Her primary method of communicating, therefore, was sufficient for her needs and she did not have to think about it rationally. She simply experienced nature flowing and reverberating through her. Everything was about her as she reveled in her me-ness. She was loving, engaging, usually self-serving and socially self-centered. In a manner of speaking, she was regal. *Meow Me Now*; it's all about me.

Despite our more complicated brain structure as human beings, we too, have a trace of Thrush in us. It is the old base brain generated "Me" button. At one psychic level we are as self-absorbed as Thrush, but often conceal that me-ness that Thrush displayed with such pride and confidence.

This is very true in matters of love. We conceal our me-ness in order to soften or minimize the potential rejection we have often previously experienced and fear meeting again. We enact this self-protective vigilance in response to our basal ganglia neurons streaming dopamine and opioids as we become smitten by love. In passionate matters of love, the metaphors of the Greek gods, *Eros* and *Ate*, aptly describe the driving, energetic arousal that occurs as an intense pulsation in the heart region, thrusting us into this excitable state. We experience ecstatic joy, a rumble and thunder. This dominating, primary communication state of mind eventually recedes and subsides as we resume our cloak of protection, that is, our rational secondary modes of communication. Eventually, our brain's serotonin helps us to recall the joy and madness of that arousing experience as we attempt to make sense in our mind about what transpired. Even when we try to delude ourselves as to what attracts and arouses in this primary communication mode of relating in matters of love, things are never exactly the same after we experience this physical and psychic awakening. As we resume our regular routines we continue to live our life on a reality-oriented, physical plane at the same time joyfully being aware of our exhilarating expressions of love, our inner me-ness and our intense desire to share it.

8.

PSYCHOLGY, BREATHING AND BODILY MOVEMENT PATTERNS

DIALOGING WITH SCOTT:
CONNECTING TO LOVE AND RESTORATIVE ENERGY PATTERNS

"Come in," I said to a tall, husky young veteran. His bootlaces were undone, his clothing hung untidily on his frame, fly unbuttoned and belt half buckled. His bulging blue eyes were watery. He was carrying a large cup of coffee in his hand. It seemed as if he had not been awake for long. My task was to evaluate him for a stress disorder. Within seconds I began to experience an intense headache. "What is this about?" I said to myself as Scott thumped himself down in a chair.

"Do you have a headache?" I asked.

Scott pointed to the front area of his head.

"We both have a headache."

This therapeutic contact began with a body-related primary communication transaction, a headache. The sensory systems of both the patient and the therapist were in contact with this primary signal or mode of communication. This was a symptom that was immediately present and manifested in both of us.

"Let's see what the story is behind these headaches," I said as we began discussing an incident in Iraq in which Scott was tossed about in a Humvee crash as the result of an IED (improvised explosive device). When he finished describing the incident I checked in with him about his headache. Mine had disappeared. So had his. Acknowledging bodily symptoms, such as a headache, while telling the story releases both the tension and the symptom.

Scott related his experience of how he got blasted by a suicide bomber who drove his vehicle into a building that Scott was walking into. He knew he was out for a while, but when he awoke he began to take care of other more seriously wounded people. "They needed more attention," was his view at the time.

Scott returned stateside. He thought his psychic pain would go away. He had been evaluated by a neurologist for a possible TBI (traumatic brain injury) from the blasts. The results were inconclusive. We talked a lot about hits to the body in athletic competition. Scott smiled as he related some of his hockey jock experiences in high school and college. He had taken a few blows to his head in the intense encounters of ice hockey games, but he said the blasts in Iraq were something else. Just after returning home, he started experiencing night terrors, sweats, panic and a racing heart beat on a daily basis. He kept thinking and feeling that he was about to die as the noise from the blasts rocked his nightmare mind. Restful sleep was hard to find.

Amy, his fiancée, had stood by him during his deployment to Iraq, but left him a few months after he came home because she could not tolerate his mood swings and emotional unavailability to her. He was argumentative, moody and whining. He hated everyone, including himself, and began to withdraw from social situations. To make matters worse, he began using alcohol to try to numb the pain. His amorous functioning ceased. He lost his loving feelings.

"My dick is dead," he confessed in a tearful, whispering voice.

Listening to Scott in an empathic manner enabled me to help him refocus his energies as he channeled a path into his inner psychic sensory system, released tension and connected to the psychic core of his inner self. This is primary communication.

"Go back to the gym." I said.

"I'll try."

"Can you talk to your primary therapists?"

"I sense they don't like me. They don't want to listen. They have ideas that they try to push on me."

"Give them a shot. Let your body heal. Learn to breathe again. You haven't been on skates in a while."

"I know," he replied with a warm smile.

Ice skating is a primary mode of communicating. It connected Scott to his primary, body-related, restorative energetic patterns emanating from his sacral core.

"One other matter, drink water when you feel like drinking beer. You will start to feel a lot better."

This was the same hypnotic command that I had heard from Thrush, the mother of my boyhood buddy.

Scott replied, "Thanks for giving me hope and some direction. Is this just a one shot deal?"

"Yes," I told him with a smile. "We did a lot. You won't forget the time we spent."

"I sure won't. Thanks."

Ten minutes later. A knock on my office door. Scott asked a question. It was really about nothing. This had been a primary communication event where the words were very secondary to the dynamics of breathing and relaxation that occurred during the session. Scott was in a trance-like, psychic healing state for which he was seeking closure. There had been a spontaneous, authentic, primary connection in our consultation. Our eyes meet. Scott exhaled with a deep breath that he had learned in the relaxation exercise with me. We warmly shook hands.

"It's hard to say goodbye. I will walk you to the door. Your dad is waiting for you."

Individuals are naturally drawn to persons who can access and activate their natural, energetic expressions and quest for positive energy. Scott and I walked out to the foyer as he waved a warm good-bye again.

His eyes had become bright. He walked in a tall, erect, posture. His chest was puffed out. He had reconnected to his

natural inner-self and core. The healing was not in the words, but
in the emotional contact that enabled Scott to safely feel in touch
with his primary self. He could then access his natural, holistic,
healing brain energies. He began to tune into his thinking-self,
his feeling-self and his sensing-self. In that moment, for only
a second or two, he felt whole. He began to recall and employ
his own inner resources, which had not disappeared, but just
been overlaid with intense stress. His symptoms would not
completely disappear overnight, but he had acquired tools for
reconnecting to his natural psychic self. He would carry with
him from our session this new awareness and a hope for the
future that he will be OK.

PSYCHOLOGY, BREATHING AND NATURE'S ENERGETIC FLOW

How did I relate to Scott? How did focusing on his
breathing help him? How long have people been
paying attention to their breath? What does breath have to
do with the origin of the name psychology? It may be hard to
believe, but the origin of psychology goes back to the Greeks
who used the term *psyche*, meaning the breath that generates the
life force energy fields that flow through us. They considered
that life begins its flow as we inhale our first breath and expires
as we exhale our last breath. Remember our injured warrior hero
Frankie's description of his breath seeming to leave him as he
struggled to breathe following his severe shrapnel wounds?

The Romans used the word *animus*, the Latin word for
breath, for anyone who inhales and exhales this life force energy.
They viewed human beings as rational animals that both breathe
and think. Our personality (from the Latin *per-* through, *son-*
sound) is the way each of us expresses the vibrational sounds of
the life force energy field. We all have flowing through us our
own unique melodic expression of that resonating breath sound.
It is in this process of inhaling and exhaling nature's life force
energy as we interact with our environment that the complexities

of the biological and psychic aspects of love originate.

The science of psychology would not actually become a field of independent study until the eighteenth century. As earlier cultures altered and evolved, each generation continued to create definitions and explanations of this vital force energy. Each new metaphor or explanation was thought to add greater enlightenment in explaining the mind or psyche. In matters of love, the goddess-driven, energetic trance state that overtakes and activates our love life was called *ate* and our creative infusions of energy were called *menos*. In the early stages of exploring the nature of the mind many diverse, indeed conflicting, speculations were proposed. Where is this psyche or mind located? One would think it is in the body. Or is it? Could it be in some other sphere or space? What is it made of? Is it just breath or something else? What does this have to do with love and relationships?

The philosophers of old stated that our view of the world and love relates to our psychology of the mind. The nature of how we know what we know, in more technical terms, is called epistemology. For example, Plato was both an idealist and a rationalist. He proposed the brain as the central organ from which our thinking-self derived its power to perceive and reflect on our biological, erotic drives. Aristotle, on the other hand, stated that the heart is the major organ of the psyche because it is where love is felt. Some of the ancient Eastern psychic-science practitioners focused on the energy churning beneath our sitting bones and the muscles in our pelvic floor. Freud shocked the world with his biological, reductionist focus on sexuality as the major driving force motivating human expression.

These formulations and opposing views have been matters for heated discussions throughout the centuries. Present day neuroscientists continue these explorations. No clear-cut scientific instruments have been devised to measure our psyche or energetic life force. Instruments that map the brain have created much excitement, even to the point of speculation that the mind can be equated with the brain. In truth, however, this great life force is still mysterious and elusive.

My psychobiological behavioral approach is to examine the effects of these mysterious pulsating and expressive, non-verbal communication energy fields as we interact and engage in the world during our multiple activities of daily living. Our physical breath and unique bodily signature expressions display our feelings and attitudes and provide some scientific data for what is happening for us. How we view ourselves may not be the same as others see us. Hormonal energies mixing with our rational and emotional brain heavily influence our behavior and thinking. Is this what love is all about? Labeling can be helpful, but can be overtaken by a biological, expressive need. Naming some need or behavior does not necessarily tame it. Exploring and discovering who we are through our relationships and love quests make living life an adventure. What love is all about is for each of us to decide.

SCIENTIFIC AND PHILOSOSPHICAL PERSPECTIVES ON MATTERS OF LOVE

Rene Descartes is credited with being the father of a scientific approach to psychology. Plato, however, is often described as the founder of philosophical psychology. He was the great master of describing the attraction and love that is man's friend, as well as his foe, his energizer and depressor, his true bipolar self. In his dialogues he describes his concepts of the mind and the irrational aspects related to love. He proposes that, as mature human beings, we must train and contain the flow of our often conflicting, energetic passions and out of control motor movements in order to master and transform this arousing love stimulation. Man is a puppet, a creature on a string. His emotions of fear, joy, pleasure and pain pull him about and make him dance to their tune. Man's task is to recognize and master these mysterious, conflicting energies that are vying for expression. It is only through death that man can resume his true nature, which is that of being a perfect spirit unhindered by the demands of a physical body. Do we have choice in these matters? The answer to this question is a matter of conjecture.

In regard to illnesses and the relationship of the body to the mind, the Greeks sought an explanation of natural, physical illnesses, as opposed to mind-related (psychological) illnesses that were thought to have originated from the gods. They knew that when the body has damage, so does the mind. Our present-day explanation would focus on brain-related impairments, such as the damage to neurons that occurs in many of our wounded marines and soldiers who have incurred traumatic brain injuries from improvised explosive devices while they were serving in Iraq. My interview with Scott demonstrates that it is often difficult to determine whether we can identify and locate the effects of discernible physical damage and/or psychological symptoms from these very traumatic physical and emotionally-related IED blasts. They are most often interrelated, one setting off the other.

MASTERING AND CONTAINIING UNBRIDLED ENERGY FIELD EXPRESSIONS

Why was ice-skating so important for Scott? Did the sports he played and the skills he developed in his youth help him survive and cope with the IED blast he encountered in Iraq? Do you recall Frankie, our wounded warrior, and how his fine-tuned baseball skills helped him survive the mortar attack on his base in Vietnam? How do all these discussions about our neurokinetic, expressive energy patterns, whether we are a righty or a lefty and how we express our other bodily-related motor movements serve us? Is there a strong relationship between motor movements and other behaviors such as dancing and sexual arousal? Do our breathing patterns influence our motor skills, how we feel about ourselves and provide the energy to motivate us to look attractive? It can be so exciting to play and win, so deflating to lose. These pulsating body movements generate the energy for the major attraction and psychic bonding we are seeking in our quest to achieve our happiness and fulfillment. Why are we so attracted to the energetic feats and accomplishments of athletes and to dancing and the rhythm of musical sounds?

In spite of all our research in the area of motor learning and expression, we still are searching for scientific explanations that describe this mysterious behavior. We do know, however, that how we swagger, pose and posture reflect our base brain's expressive motor or exhibitionistic patterns. Our personality displays are much more genuine and transparent when our bodily expressions flowing from our pelvic core resonate with the musical rhythms of our breath. Love is all about accessing and feeling this energy as it pulsates throughout our entire being. A major component of our schooling and learning goals is to teach our students skills to contain their developing neurons and to develop strategies to master these exciting, and sometimes painfully unwelcome, motor movements.

During my classes I frequently discuss this often neglected movement component of our personality patterns in which a child's motor expressions and reactions to this behavior have to be processed, developed and contained. One of my graduate school students, Loretta, shared with the class her Montessori-oriented approaches to help young preschoolers acquire skills in containing aggression and developing social behavior. She arranged a corner area of her classroom with a table and chairs and pictures of children displaying feelings of joy, sadness, anger and other emotions that she called the peace table. When there is conflict or a child just needs a few moments to be alone, this is the place to go.

One joyous moment occurred in her class when David

was upset with John and asked to take him to the peace table. Loretta slowly and calmly encouraged David to sit silently and compose himself as she initiated a breathing exercise. In her calming manner she intoned, "In...out...in...out...in...out." To everyone's surprise as David was breathing out a gigantic yawn appeared. He immediately started laughing. Loretta laughed that was not a breath out, but a dinosaur's yawn. David replied, "Well, it worked."

David's playmate John's major problem in school was he had a hard time in containing his penchant for wanting to wrestle and punch other lads. After a situation occurred at recess Loretta immediately took him to discuss the matter at the peace table. She asked him why he pushed.

"I don't know. I just couldn't stop my body from pushing. I tried, but I just couldn't stop. I knew I was going to do it, but my body just didn't stop when I told it to."

Loretta told him she was proud of him for realizing this and to talk about it with her. Then she asked him if he could think of something else to push when that feeling came over him. John thought for a few seconds, "The wall." Loretta agreed. They explored the classroom for a safe area. He named it "the punch place." Together they planned that when John felt that pushing, punching feeling coming on, he should get up and go to his punch place and push until the feeling went away.

John loved this new strategy for containing the unwanted energy surging through his body, but unexpectedly punched David the following week. David was upset and ready to strike back when John blocked his punch and with a sheepish smile laughingly said, "Use the words." John, of course, was projecting his own need to "use the words" onto David in order for himself to contain, master, observe and make changes in his own behavior. This kind of intervention teaches our young children mastery skills and strategies for containing their exciting, and sometimes painfully unwelcome, developmental motor movements.

Since the beginning of time cultures have been fascinated with these natural pulsating rhythms and sounds flowing through us. The Greeks believed this energy field to be under the influence of the god Dionysius. They would invoke his favor or energy field as they danced and released their tensions and disappointments in matters of living and love. The flute and the kettledrum were the musical instruments used to activate the excitement and energy for an ecstatic dance experience that would clean the mind and body from all tensions. Spazzing, rapid heartbeat, wailing and heavy breathing would often accompany this frenzied dancing. This altered state of consciousness resulted in emotional completeness, joy, and gladness, as time and place would fade into a mysterious tranquil and blissful space. These dancing festivals were scheduled at special times, for it took days to return to one's everyday self.

Dancing practices continued in many cultures for centuries. During the Middle Ages outbreaks of this disruptive trance-like, maniacal dancing would overtake groups of people for days. These mysterious dancing patterns were believed to fall under the auspices of St. Vitus, thus referring to this out of control behavior as St. Vitus Dance.

We are a vicariously participating culture. Our modern social media, technological repackaging of music and motor movements confirms the adage, *the more things change, the more they stay the same*. The arousing sounds of our modern day concerts and dances soothe, excite and connect us to those natural sounds reverberating through us. The musical rhythms of our favorite performers can trance us into an inner psychic godlike state as we can vicariously dance and sing along to nature's reverberating pulsations and sounds flowing through us. The excitement of the Super Bowl is one annual group cultural old base-driven ritual to determine who is the champion— Number One. After all, fans are really *fanatics* looking to join and feel that they are The Best, if only for a short period of time. In order to win in sporting events, someone has to lose. The sorrow of the loser energizes the joy of the winner.

CONTROVERSIES SURROUNDING ENERGY FIELD EROTIC EXPRESSIONS

Long before the time of the great physician, Paracelsus (1493–1541 AD), health care practitioners were attempting to identify the physical causes of these expressions of wild dancing that erotically arouse us, release tension and operate outside our conscious control. What we do know is that some brain-generated movements are voluntary (pyramidal system) and others involuntary (extrapyramidal system). Dr. Paul MacLean, pioneer brain scientist, concluded in his monumental text, *The Triune Brain in Evolution*, that all the research studies about motor movements fail to scientifically define the brain's exact function. We continue to explore this mystery, just as some scientists are still looking to discover the *grandmother cell* that connects the mind to the body. We can create terms for these surging, and sometimes unwelcome, energetic expressions and even harness them with the many dampening medications that are able to take the edge off their intensity, but we still don't know a lot about these paradoxical complexities that can make us excited at one time and lethargic another. Experiencing these motor movement energy patterns can result in a heavenly or hellish outcome.

MY PERSPECTIVE

I am proposing that we are naturally coping with multiple biological streams of energy patterns being manifested through our hormones and neurotransmitters. These surge and compete for physical and sexual expression. The physical component of love is manifested in these motor movement energy patterns that are driving us to act and react. Yet our psychic quest is to relate and experience an emotional closeness with our beloved that lasts forever. When we are operating in an analytic manner, our hormonal energies are mostly contained or restrained. Yet these mysteriously driven, primary communication energy patterns sit in the deep recesses of our brain, not that far removed from our awareness. Too many emotional and intense expressions of love and attraction can also be overwhelming for a potential lover to handle and as a result flood them with emotional brain-generated protective anxiety. Mastering our thrilling bodily sensations and the anticipatory excitement of new adventures with our present or potential new lover makes us feel ecstatic and connected to this mysterious, moving, creative energy field flowing through us.

Successful reciprocal and enchanting romantic relationships can be enhanced when we are tuned into the sensations flowing throughout our body, particularly the breathing patterns and physical movements that are related to nature's energy patterns seeking expression. How we communicate our needs during our interactions with people defines our personality style and views about life. Individuals who relate to the world in an answer-seeking, information-oriented way of interacting with people have a tendency to be constantly analyzing motivational patterns as they look for reasons. This intellectual approach numbs the powerful, bodily-movement sensations that are being transmitted from their primary non-verbal emotional brain. In this pseudo-scientific manner of relating they are surreptitiously seeking and sucking energy. They are unconsciously searching for situations in which they can release the physical and psychic knots that are limiting and impairing their quest for emotional recognition, engagement and love.

Love is so overpowering. Attraction can highly excite us. It can also scare us. Anxiety arrives. When these emotional sensations overtake us we feel ourselves losing control. Our mind rattles as our familiar way of seeing things is in the process of crumbling. We yearn for love, but sometimes it can be too much to take.

Our sexually expressive, primitive old brain's creative and destructive motor movements churning through our body's pelvic core area continue to remain a mystery despite many inconclusive scientific speculations. What we do know is we all have a hungry heart that pulsates and draws us to seek out individuals who can connect to us and share with us the feelings of love and joy resonating deep within us.

9.

MATTERS OF LOVE:
MIND–BODY APPROACHES AND DISPUTES

ANCIENT THERAPEUTIC METHODS FOR TREATING
LOVESICKNESS

Do you remember Jenny and Chauncey's story and Jenny's therapeutic approach to healing the forlorn patient? Jenny had a full-blown confidence in herself, a strong, positive self-image. She enthusiastically believed that her therapeutic sexual treatment would improve Chauncey's quality of life. This was the same cure proposed by the ancient Greek, Roman and Arabic healers 2,500 years ago. In those days it was considered a prescriptive method for healing love sickness.

Jenny had probably not read Claudius Galen's (131c.–201 AD) account of love sickness. He described victims of this illness as individuals who are unhappy and anxious. Their sleep is restless as they suddenly awaken. They experience major mood fluctuations, feeling euphoric at one moment and utterly miserable the next. Galen attributed the physical cause for a sullen, lovesick person to black bile. Rufus of Ephesus, who lived a generation before Galen, had recommended therapeutic intercourse as a remedy for treating this problem. Jenny was attempting to relate to Chauncey with methods that she felt intuitively. How many mental health professionals know about these ancient methods that were shunned by the newly formed Christian church?

Remember the neurokinetic energy field test in chapter four where you determined your orientation to left- or right-handed preferences? The healers from ancient Egypt and Greece also knew about another variation of this mysterious energetic phenomenon that they called the pulse test. The healer would hold the arm of the patient and observe the vibrating pulse, as she or he would mention the names of persons for whom there could be strong romantic feelings. The patient's pulse would surge when a significant name was mentioned. A secret love would be uncovered. How to deal with this love sickness phenomenon went to sleep in the Western world for a thousand years until the Arab world's treatise on love sickness was translated by Constantine the African in the eleventh century.

Can you recall the stories of love that I wrote about in the second chapter about Cameron, Claude, Corrine and June and their experiences in Iraq? I was their age when I served on active duty in the navy. Please do not delude yourself into thinking that the "newer therapies" are more effective than Dr. Semrad's model of seeking and finding love, a treatment approach that had been used in other wars. Present psychotherapeutic treatment approaches tend to ignore the combatants' unique, neurokinetic, love searching energy that is such an important therapeutic factor in their recovery. That old brain F-sound that had continuously reverberated throughout my group of navy corpsmen is still transmitting its energy despite the philosophical, pseudo-psychological attempts to ignore its existence.

ELEVATING EROTIC ENERGY: CHRISTIAN PASSIONATE LOVE

Not so long ago, a young monk confessed to me that when he went to the altar to receive Holy Communion he experienced an intense love for Jesus. He would become so excited that he experienced a full erection. His penis would throb in wild excitement and, embarrassingly, he would ejaculate upon reception of the sacrament. There could be several explanations for this event, but suffice it to say he embraced Christ Jesus in every manner, both physically and spiritually, in his mind and body. He became one with him in life and death. Mary

Magdalene was a passionate lover of Christ. She had no fear of expressing her physical self to the Great One. Young John, the apostle, was referred to as "The Beloved."

The theologians in the early church attempted to contain and harness the many "unacceptable" practices of sexual expression that were rampant in the early centuries of the Christian church. They promoted Socrates' discussion in the *Phaedrus* that a sublimated, *tantric* love generates high levels of psychic energy. This devotion, commitment and dedication to the God man required total surrender and trust by the mystic.

Juliana of Mont-Cornillon developed an intense yearning to be united with Jesus and, like the young monk, was obsessed with contacting Jesus in the reception of the sacrament. During this period of her life she was viewed as being psychotic, but emerged from her trance totally transformed as a psychic healer and abbess. She even persuaded the church authorities to initiate the special feast of *Corpus Christi* (Body of Christ) to celebrate this psychically powerful devotional ritual. The saintly Thomas Aquinas composed an exhilarating chant, *"Panis Angelicus,"* "The Bread of Angels," to celebrate this new feast.

If you can shut down your analytic brain for a short while, tune into your emotional neurokinetic musical energy and pulse it with someone who has the same type of devotion for this or any other elevating musical event, the energy will alter your obsessing mind and cleanse your thinking brain from all your petty grudges. If you are just intellectualizing or analyzing it, you are ignoring and abstracting yourself from contacting and accessing the energy and so become dismissive or bored because it does not fit into your way of seeing the world. The beauty of being a human being is that the world is really about you and how you tune in with your musical energetic flow to people and situations with which you wish to share your joy and passion.

CONSTANTINE THE AFRICAN'S PRESCRIPTIVE LOVE-MAKING TREATISE

During the tumultuous early Renaissance period the writings of Avicenna (980-1037 AD) were translated into Latin by Constantine the African. Thomas Aquinas, my college philosophy hero, was a direct recipient of these documents and composed the great *Summa*. Avicenna's treatise, *Ishk*, postulated that love is driven by an individual's need to connect and be related to love, perfection and beauty. His treatment for this love sickness is the same as that prescribed by Galen and Rufus of Ephesus, that is, engage in sexual activity. We saw that in Claude's attraction to the beautiful Maria.

The mysterious Constantine the African arrived at the monastery of Montecassino in Italy in the middle of the eleventh century. It was thought that he came from North Africa. What is known is that he arrived at the monastery with a trunk load of Arabic medical texts. One of the authors was Avicenna. Constantine advocated the prescriptive lovemaking methods of Avicenna, and, being in the company of monks and religious people, he recommended other remedies as well, such as drinking good wine, chanting the name of God and making good friends. Constantine integrated the Eastern healing methodologies for treating love-seeking sickness with the philosophical-psychic approaches that had been well known to the Western world since Plato's era. He translated the Arabic works on love, madness and love-sickness into Latin and named his work the *Viaticum*. He intended this small pamphlet to provide comfort and guidance for the wandering pilgrim to take with him on his journey. This treatise on love, however, had a profound effect on theologians and love-seekers for several centuries. Many theologians wrote commentaries on the prescription offered in this work, to seek someone with whom to share inner psychic love on a physical and spiritual plane. One of these interpreters was Peter of Spain

(1205–1277 AD) who eventually became Pope John XXI.

RELIGIOUS BATTLES AND THE MADNESS OF THE MIND

Love has its ways of creating and renewing life. In reaction to challenges to its authority and the emergence of reformative religious practices and beliefs, the church was intent on formalizing strict rules and regulations and designing rituals for containing what is considered today to be psychotic maladapted behaviors of the mind. The abbess, Teresa of Avila (1545–1582 AD), introduced natural biological explanations for the visions her nuns were experiencing, such as minds wandering and crazy thoughts from dream-like states. She proposed that body behavior states could be influenced by emotions and moods. She convinced the Inquisitors that people who experience extraordinary alterations in consciousness, such as visions or what we would call hallucinations today, should be treated as if they were ill. Teresa was able to alter the prevalent perspective on visions to an acceptance of these behaviors as the result of a person being a victim or creature of nature, rather than being someone who was acting in a free, consenting and responsible manner. These were ill people who were in need of help, not punishment. Teresa and her followers were still persecuted by traditionalist leaders who were resistant to her newly formulated psychological–spiritual practices because they were unable to verify intellectually the psychic experiences of these mystics.

Teresa's great and lasting achievement was to refine the evaluation of religious experiences and visions. She initiated a shift from theological explanations to a more natural view of the mind and altered states of consciousness. These visions were no longer viewed as originating from the devil, but rather from some psychophysical inner disturbance. As a result of these newly reformulated conceptualizations, the medical views of Galen in regard to mental illness were resurrected. He had formulated

151

that when there was an excess of black bile in the body it produced melancholy and mania resulting in an impairment of imagination and reasoning. Slowly, an empirical view of man was beginning to develop, challenging the formal, standardized thinking of the day. We are really no different today, with all our political correctness and well-intentioned and pseudo-scientifically proper way to behave and rule-making that occurs.

People in villages, in castles, and in monasteries, however, were breaking away from the structures of church-sanctioned thought and beliefs. Michelangelo had been secretly dissecting cadavers to create and refine his sculpting. The drawings of Leonardo da Vinci (1452–1519 AD) also created great interest in the structure and function of the human body. Vesalius had used Avicenna's writings to introduce the science of anatomy. Views of the mind and its functional relationship with the body were in the process of changing as a result of this emerging knowledge of the physical body. These early beginnings of anatomical science were often met, not only with resistance, but also with physical danger for their authors. Vesalius himself was prosecuted by the Inquisitors and charged with murder, when during a vivisection of one of his deceased patients, the heart was seen to be still beating. He was able to negotiate a penance to amend his wrongful action by making a pilgrimage to the Holy Land. Unfortunately, on this journey he died in a shipwreck off the Grecian coast.

A NEW BEGINNING: MODERN APPROACHES TO SCIENCE AND HEALTH

With the emergence of cultural shifts during the sixteenth century and the resulting changes in thinking styles, the many conceptualizations of the mind–body relationship underwent radical challenges and changes. The inventions of the printing press and the mechanical clock were providing the framework for man to evaluate himself in a scientific, rather than spiritual manner. My adolescent hero, a recovered, seriously wounded soldier and founder of the Jesuit order, Ignatius (1491–1556 AD), was already promoting change by redesigning methods for education and scientific investigations. All these years later, Francis is the first Jesuit pope.

Rene Descartes (1596–1650 AD), a Jesuit-educated philosopher of science, stated that it was necessary to make a distinction between the mind and body in order to examine the nature of matters that are both spiritual and physical. He believed that the soul or spirit of man was "one and indivisible," and stated that the body and the brain should be investigated as machines. He proposed the metaphor of the clock as a resolution of the mind–body dilemma. During the middle ages the clockmaker was held in high esteem. The clock was viewed as a mechanical machine that operated by the motion of its weights and wheels and thus functioned independently of its designer or maker. Descartes considered man to be like a clock, created by God and yet operating at a distance from his Maker.

Descartes created several other metaphors to describe the relationship between the mind and the body. The veins were organ pipes, the nerves were strings, and the heart was a spring. This was the beginning of the use of physical metaphors to explain empirical and psychic phenomena. As a result, man began to alter his previous conceptualization of the life force and animal spirits running through the body that had been in existence since the times of Hypocrites and reformulated by Galen.

Human malaise and disease had been thought to originate from an imbalance in four basic substances called our humors or vital fluids. Diseases were considered to be brought on by vapors in the air that were inhaled. Some health practitioners continue to employ a modified version of this approach that postulates a person can experience symptoms when their humors are out of balance. There are four basic elements: *earth* present in black bile, *fire* in yellow bile, *water* in phlegm, and *air* in the blood. These four vital fluids are present in some degree in the blood stream.

Moods or temperaments are also related to these basic elements. A depressed or sad person's temperament is related to *black bile*. An agitated, angry, restless person is labeled choleric (*yellow bile*). A calm, not easily moved person is considered *phlegmatic (water). A happy, hopeful, cheerful person is called sanguine* (blood). During this era it was thought that rotting organic matter and evil spirits were invading the atmosphere, affecting our personalities and causing disease. One of the major medical treatment approaches was bloodletting to balance the humors and bring the body into harmony with nature. Words such as humor, phlegmatic and temper are commonplace words in our vocabulary today. Ayurvedic medicine, which originated in India, is still based on most of these same humors. Massage, yoga, acupuncture and meditative practices date from these times.

Descartes refined the views of life that prevailed in his time. His psychological conception of man's sensations, perceptual capacities and altered states of consciousness as they relate to eye movements, breathing and imagination, have inspired scientific inquiries even to this present day. It could be safely concluded that Descartes' newly designed approaches contributed to the Western scientific method of evaluating the human body and psyche in an objective, scientific and empirical fashion. His philosophical approach disconnected man from the life force and psychic energy fields and redefined him with cognitive and empirical constructs. Psychology became a study and not an experience.

In addition to being known for his many mathematical and scientific pursuits, Descartes also had the reputation of being quite temperamental and was involved in several romantic encounters. Descartes' mother had died when he was an infant. While he was living in the Dutch Republic, he married Helena and had a daughter, Francine. He became forlorn when Francine died at the age of five and Helena shortly thereafter. A close friend provided some consolation when he facilitated an introduction for Descartes to Princess Elizabeth of Bohemia, the granddaughter of King James I of England. An intensely platonic romantic correspondence with Elizabeth provided the exciting spark for his famous psychological treatise, *Passions of the Soul*. Queen Christina of Sweden had been a student of the love gods and goddesses of ancient Greece and became interested in his treatise. She invited Descartes to meet and tutor her. He accepted the invitation with the expectation that Elizabeth would also be invited. Perhaps she and Christina would become friends and she would restore some of Elizabeth's family's lost territories. It did not happen. As we all know, in matters of love, politics and competition for affection and supremacy are dominant human drives.

Christina's and Descartes' emotional connection and lifestyle were not in sync. Her early and his late schedule resulted in lots of turmoil. Sessions had to begin early in the morning. Descartes was also pursuing his scientific interests during his time in Stockholm. In his heart he had failed in his romantic pursuit to please Elizabeth. He became ill with pneumonia and died in Stockholm. The cause of his death remains a mystery. Some say his pneumonia was not serious enough to result in his death. Conjectures have arisen varying from the intense stress of Christina's insistent demands, to a broken heart for failing Elizabeth, and even to the Grand Inquisitor's persecution of him for his heretical views.

With this introduction to modern science, life force energies were no longer viewed in terms of love, but were rather defined in concrete, demonstrable terms. A dichotomy of mind and body was introduced. It still prevails. The assumption now became that the mind can be objectified into physical empirically validated biological and behavioral variables. Eventually, during the nineteenth century a newly formed inner psychic science field was instituted with the introduction of hypnosis and healing trance practices in order to account for the unexplainable, nonscientific aspects of human behavior. Meanwhile, brain scientists ignored this component of man and pursued their empirical physical investigations of the brain. This held great appeal for individuals who wanted to explore the demonstrable components of a human being.

Descartes had begun the quest that has continued ever since to discover the "grandmother cell" that connects the mind to the body. Most of the research scientists who were inspired by Descartes investigated the anatomy and physiology of the brain. They continue to employ cognitive, scientific methods and accordingly do not focus on matters of the heart, love and relationships. A history of these investigations, the controversies and the findings of the many pioneer brain scientists are presented in the notes and reference section at the end of the book.

Investigators still continue to attempt to describe the nature of man in objective replicable and physical measures of the brain and body. These information-oriented, data seeking approaches do little, however, to enlighten us in our inquiry into the mysteries of love and the needs of our human heart, the psychic aspect of man, and how to utilize, explore, and contain this mysterious aspect of our human nature.

PASSION AND COMMITMENT: INITIATING CHANGE

A serious problem existed in Europe and the United States during the middle of the eighteenth century. Women who had given birth often died as a result of childbed fever (puerperal fever). Oliver Wendell Holmes (1809–1895 AD), a Boston physician and essayist, observed that an obstetrician had died one week after performing an autopsy on a woman who had died from childbed fever. Holmes thoroughly investigated and concluded that doctors should wash their hands to prevent transmissions of puerperal fever. In 1843 he presented his observations and recommendations at a symposium. He eventually published a pamphlet asserting that doctors with unwashed hands were transmitting the disease from patient to patient. Dr. Holmes was criticized and ridiculed by experts in the field for his hand washing suggestion because it was not considered evidenced-based, just his personal musings.

In 1846 there were two independently functioning maternity wards in the same hospital where a young resident, Ignaz Semmelweis, a Hungarian native who was educated in Vienna, began his obstetrical training. He observed that women who delivered their babies under the care of doctors had a substantially greater risk of dying during childbirth than those women who gave birth with the assistance of midwives. After examining many factors he concluded that women were dying due to the decaying tissues remaining on the hands of the doctors who were conducting autopsies in the morgue of the hospital. Their custom was to do autopsies with their students before delivering babies. The doctors would then deliver the babies without washing their hands. Ignaz ordered his subordinates to thoroughly wash their hands in a chlorine solution before they met with their patients. The death rate drastically decreased.

Most of the senior ranking doctors were quite upset. They considered Ignaz's assertions to be brazen and his admonitions to be out of line. They refused to reevaluate their methods of practice. They were steeped in their traditional, evidenced-based practices and could not consider a new perspective that was in conflict with theirs. They resented Ignaz's proposed intervention to wash your hands.

He became despondent following the rejections and ridicule he was receiving for his newly discovered findings. He took time off to travel to Venice to cope with his emotional distress and the rebukes from the senior medical establishment. When he returned to Vienna, he even became more convinced of the validity of his findings when he learned that a close friend, Jakob Kolletschka, had been accidentally poked with a student's scalpel while performing an autopsy and died. Jakob's death confirmed his belief that the poisonous, decaying tissues, that in our day would probably be called streptococcal bacteria, could infect anyone.

Ignaz's emotional brain began to flood his mind and dominate his behavior. He wrote letters to obstetricians throughout Europe urging them to wash their hands. The memories of Anton Mesmer's unscientific, magnet-healing treatments did not help them revise their thinking. They rejected and scorned Ignaz's findings, which were not scientifically congruent with their view of disease at that time.

The humors theory dating back to the times of Hippocrates and Galen was still the primary model of disease. Ignaz's senior ranking doctors were intellectually oriented and arrogantly confident in their medical practices. As a result, Ignaz was not offered a staff position at the hospital in Vienna.

Eventually, he reestablished his practice at a hospital in his native Budapest and instituted his approach with success there. Some years later he published his findings. He still had to continually endure the scorn, ridicule and rebuke by the European medical establishment. Ignaz's rage reactions intensified as he became obsessed with his quest. At times he behaved in an agitated and delusional psychotic-like fashion. He was eventually committed to a mental hospital. Fourteen days later he died at the age of forty-seven. His autopsy indicated that he had died from a severe beating received from the attendants working in the hospital. Unfortunately, Ignaz had become intensely emotionally overwhelmed, and obsessed with his discovery and was unable to refute his critics in the manner of Dr. Holmes, who had admonished, "If there is voluntary blindness, any interested oversight, any culpable negligence, even, in such a matter, and the facts shall reach the public ear; the pestilence-carrier of the lying-in chamber must look to God for pardon, for man will never forgive him."

It would not be until the mid 1860s that the research findings of Louis Pasteur demonstrated the germ theory of disease, that microorganisms are the true cause of many diseases. This explained Ignaz's observations and interventions. Oliver Wendell Holmes had visited with Pasteur in France to discuss their mutual interests. In the British Isles, Joseph Lister was able to integrate these new discoveries. He had been struggling to develop effective surgical procedures. The findings of Pasteur inspired him to introduce carbonic acid to reduce infection. He also initiated sterile techniques of washing hands, using gauze and wearing gloves that resulted in successful surgical outcomes. Centuries old medical thinking had been totally transformed and reformed by these dedicated heroes. Dr. Lister was knighted for his findings, but unfortunately spent the last ten years of his life in a melancholic state; his wife, the love of his life, had passed away.

Dr. Ignaz Semmelweis would eventually be honored as a medical pioneer and received many posthumous accolades for saving the lives of many mothers. A memorial statue sits in his native city of Budapest honoring this dedicated physician who devoted his life to saving lives, daring to be right, daring to be true and standing like a hero even unto his death.

A PULITZER PRIZE GONE ASTRAY: LOCATING THE GRANDMOTHER CELL IN THE BRAIN

With this introduction to modern science, neurokinetic expressions of life force energies were no longer viewed in terms of Galen's breathing and love energy, but were rather defined in concrete demonstrable terms. They had to be observable. The assumption now became that the mind can be objectified into physical, empirically validated, biological and behavioral variables. This approach created the field of brain science that began our continuing quest to discover the grandmother cell that connects the mind to the body. The notes and reference section at the end of the book discusses the scientific investigations into the nature of the body and mind.

Our modern day perspective has best been presented by Dr. Paul MacLean (1913–2007 AD) who proposed that the course of evolution of the human brain developed along three patterns that differ from each other in many ways. He employed the term reptilian to describe the first tier forebrain. This part of the brain has control over instinctual behavior, social pecking orders, rituals, and compulsions. The second tier brain, the limbic system, is linked into emotional expression, including sexual and aggressive behavior. The third tier brain is the neocortical brain devoted to reading, talking and counting. It is our problem solving brain. MacLean named the smell and taste areas of the brain the limbic system. This part of the brain, together with the old reptilian brain, does not have a language to express itself, but communicates nonverbally through signs and signals. There are no real words to label nonverbal signs and signals that directly, but unconsciously, affect our emotional thinking. The major modes of expression for these old brain states are metaphors, analogies and expletives. MacLean's findings and formulations concerning the emotional brain continue to be the dominant model in man's pursuit of explaining mind–body phenomena.

In his classic book, *The Triune Brain in Evolution*, MacLean relates the story of Becky and Lucy, two chimpanzees being studied at Yale University. A surgical procedure was performed that altered the frontal lobe section of their brains. Becky developed temper tantrums and began screaming and yelling, defecating and urinating on a regular basis. Following another procedure on her frontal lobes, Becky was left in such a state that she no longer cared. She showed little enthusiasm for living. She appeared to withdraw from everything.

Dr. Fulton and his collaborators in this research study were so enthused about their ability to alter Becky's behavior that they convinced Dr. Egas Monitz of Portugal, an outstanding professor of neurology in Lisbon, to try this procedure with human patients. The procedure was initiated with "amazing" results. The patients that received this surgery became calm and serene. As a result, Dr. Monitz was awarded the Nobel Prize in 1949 for his work in pioneering lobotomies. The mental health world became very excited by this "new revolutionary" procedure. They thought that they could regulate the mind by controlling the body. In time, they learned that this surgical treatment made patients numb, lethargic and forgetful. They could feel neither joy nor sorrow. They had no goals or aspirations. There was no future, only the empty nothingness of the present. Altering the brain altered the mind of these patients. An individual's psychological state was dramatically affected and, in a sense, damaged. Practitioners assumed that their patients felt no emotional pain. They had not bothered initially to inquire. Upon questioning and evaluating the patients' subjective states, they learned that the pain was actually worse. As with many innovations and modifications and subsequent scientific celebrations, this procedure silently disappeared, not without forever leaving its indelible mark on many patients.

A CASE EXAMPLE OF A LOBOTOMY PATIENT:

Sadie was a patient in one of my social group therapies. She was a well to-do, middle-aged woman who had married well, but suffered from a mental illness. Eventually, her husband and children separated from her, but provided her with a comfortable income. She acted, in many ways, like my cat, Thrush, whom you met in the chapter on primary communication. Sadie was totally self-involved. Her life was all about Me. She considered herself to be always right and demanded that the world interact with her on her own terms. It was part of her lifestyle to interrupt a conversation at any time. She had poor listening skills. Because of the lobotomy she had undergone in order to cure her mental illness, she could not reacquire the social skills needed to function in a normal human manner. A loss of both awareness and control of her emotions was a major residual of her procedure. She did not know that. In fact, if confronted she would act like Becky. Her demeanor was that of disdain for everyone. This protected her from any self-loathing ideation.

It was just a matter of chance that my wife was enrolled in a creative writing class at a local adult education center. She returned home from the first class, telling me that there was an intrusive woman in the class who, by continually interrupting, would not allow any exchanges between other students and the instructor. I listened to my wife for a few minutes and asked her the student's name. She confirmed my hunch. Sadie was still transacting with the world in her own unique way. Her personality pattern was the direct result of undergoing a lobotomy.

These physical measures of the brain and body that relate to our thinking self do little, however, to enlighten us in our inquiry into the sensing and feeling self needs of the human heart, the psychic component of man and how to utilize, explore, and contain this mysterious aspect of our human nature.

THE LOVE BUZZ AND HOT SPOTS IN THE BRAIN

With the arrival of new technology during these past decades, our enthusiasm to pursue our intellectual inquiries to decipher this quest for understanding the mechanisms of love has been revived. Identifying and locating hot spots in the brain has become the new fad. In the chapter about my navy days, I described opiates and neurotransmitters in the brain that I playfully termed my juices. It is not in the scope of this book to trace the history of their origin other than to state that there have been many attempts to locate and describe the pleasure centers in the brain. This all began around 1954 when Olds and Milner located a pleasure center in the septal area of the brain. They had implanted electrodes in that area and learned that rats preferred to press a lever for pleasure rather than eat or drink. The location of this area was eventually refined to a spot in the nearby nucleus accumbens. The present thinking is that dopamine is a motivating ingredient in activating expressions of love. Natural opioids are also pleasure-generating substances, but not the big deal that was earlier promulgated. These systems interact and spin off of each other in ways that confound us. Siri Leknes and her colleagues have recently reported that the same neural circuits that elicit pleasure are also connected to pain centers. If there is, indeed, a hot spot or love center in the brain it has so far eluded us.

TRANCE AND HYNOTIC STATES

It became obvious to clinical practitioners in the helping professions that this new scientific approach was not effective in dealing with the powerful energies of the old reptilian and emotional limbic brain structures that we know of today. Man became aware that he could extrapolate information from a situation and observe himself in a somewhat objective fashion with these scientific methods, but the mysterious surges of love seemed to defy logical explanations.

What do we do with these attractive and negative emotional connections between people? Practitioners began to seek psychical causes to explain this madness of love with all of its excitement and the many symptoms that resulted from unsuccessful and unrequited romantic encounters. Intellectual analysis was one treatment that had an answer for the causes of these love symptoms. There are still practitioners today who employ these methods. If you can name it, you can tame it. These analytic formulations are just words, or yups, as I would say. They do not translate into practical solutions. They just deny or avoid the mysterious neurokinetic manifestations of the base-brain described by Dr. Hughlings Jackson that continue to seep out and search for expression and connection.

So what am I talking about? Listen to the tale of Penny and Donald.

On a warm Cape Cod summer evening, as darkness began to shroud the day's activities and visibility was almost nonexistent, Penny was hanging out in the railroad yard with Donald. With only the shadowed shapes of silent train cars for company, it was not a bad spot to view the stars. There was little streetlight to distract from the luminous firmament. While crossing the tracks Penny stumbled, fell and bruised her thigh. She let out a wild-sounding yelp in reaction to the intense pain she experienced. Donald was initially stunned by the sudden shock of the accident. He composed himself by taking in a deep breath. Carefully, he began touching her gently in the chest area and then he softly squeezed her hand as he took in another deep breath.

"That pain will go away from you and into me," said Donald in a firm, but loving manner, already beginning to induce a calming, relaxing, trance-like state in Penny.

"OK! OK," cried Penny. "It will go right into you, Donny."

"Ouch!" screamed Donald. He howled and yelled.

Soon they followed the tracks to the main street of town. They found a spot to have a cool drink as the intense shock of the accident began to recede and their composure returned, allowing their attention to center on more romantic interests. Within the next hour they settled down and retired for the night.

The following morning Donald playfully asked Penny, "What do you remember about last night?"

"That thigh hurt so badly, but I was able to put it aside because of you. I know you like that hypnotic malarkey. I don't. I've got no pain now, but a black and blue," scorned Penny.

"Would you like me to get a black and blue too?" smirked Donald.

Penny laughed. "You would, too, just to play with me. Enough."

We humans have a very complex mind and psychic apparatus so that we have the skill or capacity to play, fantasize, trust and imagine. Such was the situation when Penny was in acute pain, but with a hypnotic suggestion from Donald she was able to put aside and dissociate from her pain.

A famous psychologist, Ernest "Jack" Hilgard, coined the term *hidden observer* to describe a situation in which we can be engaged in an activity in one state and at the same time can observe ourselves from a distance as we are engaged in a situation. That is, there can be different streams of energy patterns flowing in our awareness at the same time. Penny corroborated this in her dialogue with Donald as she was observing what was happening to her the entire time while she was put in a trance by Donald. Similarly, we can be carrying on a conversation with a person or group and be simultaneously reflecting on another situation. We might be thinking of an exciting, arousing, interesting person we had met the night before. Another example is, when we are being challenged or scorned, we often hold our breath so that we can compose our self, become rational and plan our response. We can be in an active mode like mowing the lawn and at the same time thinking of how nice a passive mode such as receiving a massage would be.

New body–mind treatments, including trance and *hypnosis*, were introduced as a pathway for connecting to the life force energies. Individuals that use the methods of hypnosis, exhortation or coercion, employ a simple psychological technique, that is, they tell someone to do or not to do something. Being willing to be commanded at some level by someone is a natural human trait, just as we described in our story of Penny and Donald. Attitude and expectation have so much to do with the outcome of one's experience. The closer the emotional connection, the more effective the results of the command can be. How this happens is a matter of conjecture. This magical, mysterious phenomenon involves connecting to our emotionally engaging, neurokinetic energy patterns.

Is hypnosis or trance a special state of awareness in which we have more access to the deep recesses of our mind? Yes, I think everyone would agree. How it happens, however, lends itself to multiple interpretations. Hypnotic phenomena have been present since the beginning of time. From our earliest times oracles were believed to possess the power to alter consciousness and foretell the future. As a youngster I was impressed when I read about the story of a young, mystic monk Adesius, who was a healing oracle at an ancient Greek retreat spa. He would put on a garland, look at the sun, go into a trance-like state and begin to offer advice to the visitor as if he knew everything about them. I too, have encountered Adesius-like persons at some of the monasteries and ashrams I have visited. One would not be so foolish as to deny that there is some transmuted or elevated sexual chemistry transpiring in these transactions. All groups have some erotic component to their rituals that excite participants to come back for more.

To bring us to the modern dialogue of these trance states, Dr. Thomas Hackett, the late chief of psychiatry at Harvard's Massachusetts General Hospital, claimed that the French Jesuits brought these trance practices back to France. Hypnosis was a tool that they had learned while interacting with Indian tribes in North America. Whether this is true is matter for conjecture. What is known is the story of Father Johann Gassner (1727–1779 AD). He suffered multiple illnesses in his early life and sought treatment from many sources with few results. After much contemplation, he arrived at the conclusion that his problem was psychic and that an evil spirit had to be expelled from his mind and body. He was quite successful in solving his problem, treating it with the ancient Christian ritual of exorcism, the casting out of devils.

The story of Jesus casting out devils is pervasive in early Christian history. The tale of the devil being cast into swine and rushing to the sea has been discussed for centuries. In the early Christian era, Jesus was viewed as a healer of body and soul. Sickness was viewed as an illness coming from an evil spirit. Accordingly, healing was carried out by expunging the evil one through invocation of the Christ and the Holy Spirit. This method still exists today in many religious groups. Health practitioners use it as well, but ignore the religious component. It works if you want to believe.

It was in this modality that Father Johann Gassner performed his treatment of probative exorcism. He would command the spirit to identify itself by a signal and would then command the evil one to immediately depart from the person. As a result the individual would be cleansed and healed from their illness.

Many professionals and followers from all stations of life observed Gassner as he conducted his practices. This was the Age of Enlightenment, however, and there were many observers who challenged his approach and asserted that Gassner's treatment was irrational and magical. Franz Anton Mesmer (1734–1815 AD), a highly dramatic physician in his own right, disputed Gassner's methodology and asserted that the metal crucifix that Gassner employed in his treatments contained magnets that were conducting the healing energies for his subjects. The archbishop of Salzburg, the Pope, and the Bavarian Academy of Science were looking for a rational explanation for this phenomenon. Being able to have a scientific cause can be both a friend and an enemy. They were unconsciously influenced by Mesmer's attempted rational, grandiose postulation of animal magnetism. Gassner was banished to live a life of prayer and penance.

MESMER'S TRANCE AND HYPNOTIC HEALING

Anton Mesmer had been influenced by a Jesuit astronomer, Max Hehl, who had theorized that all human beings were connected through cosmic magnetic forces. His influence was reflected in Mesmer's construct of animal magnetism, a phenomenon that was in part related to Newtonian gravitational theories of the tides and the moon. It simply stated that we are all bound or tied together by a gravitational heavenly and earthly body energy or fluid called magnetism, which kept humans in love and social contact. Sounds nice and seductive. Mesmer applied magnets to patients, feeding them with iron so the treatment would work more effectively. Patients would have convulsive attacks. Tension was released and patients experienced relief from their symptoms. These spazzing episodes became the vogue of the day. This enabled them to become romantically engaged.

People from high society were attracted to this treatment method. Mesmer was very well received in social circles in Vienna. His evidence-based research findings, no different than what is happening today, led to the "scientific conclusion" that any object that Mesmer had touched with magnets such as humans or animals, was healed by this magnetic energy. After the experimental findings of Ben Franklin about static electricity, the term was altered from magnetic to electrical forces.

For a ten-year period Mesmer enjoyed a successful practice in Vienna until the physicians termed his practice methods non-medical. He was driven out of town and reestablished himself in Paris. His therapeutic regimen consisted of sitting in front of his patients, looking fiercely into their eyes as he clasped his patient's hands with his own and then pushed his hands on the solar plexus (between the chest and belly button) of his patient. The patient would then respond by making noises and spazzing, thereby releasing physical and psychic tensions. This method was no different than some of the body–mind therapy procedures of today. My experience at Dr. M's office had many of these components, but we did not attribute pseudo-causes to our experiences.

In 1784, as a result of Mesmer's claim that he had discovered a new magnetic fluid, Louis XVI appointed an investigative commission of scientists that included Ben Franklin. Their conclusions were that there was nothing physically demonstrable to document animal magnetism, no scientific empirical evidence to support it. They postulated that the therapeutic effect was the result of suggestion and imagination. Despite these findings, Mesmer became a folk hero and this procedure became known as mesmerism.

Today, when we are entranced by a panoramic view or a beautiful face, we say we are mesmerized which keeps alive at a metaphorical level the postulations of Franz Mesmer despite the fact that they turned out to be not true. The process was valid, but the intellectual explanation (the yup) was inaccurate. Verbal explanations of this process are only metaphors and do not have corroborative physical causes. In the same way, love and its connectivity defy scientific dismemberment and elude rational cognitive explanation. Trance and hypnotic states have become the pathway for relating to the process of connecting with love.

Love can be beautifully described by lovers and poets even though we do not scientifically and intellectually know just what it is. We seem to be able to feel it, but cannot isolate it. We can capture it neither in the chemist's crucible nor in our eager hands. We can only experience it in all its splendor and mystery. And so when we need to relieve the agony of love's heartaches we eagerly search for a pathway to release our pain. Trance and hypnotic techniques can help us in this restorative process. The

Greeks were well aware of this innate need. Plato viewed poetry and dancing as non-rational, trance-like states that enable us to release the tensions of this mysterious phenomenon of love.

The lack of a scientific explanation of trance states did not lessen peoples' attraction to engaging in Mesmer's treatments. This mélange of techniques and manipulations was embraced throughout Europe and the U.S. during the nineteenth century. Magnetism eventually simply underwent a name change and reframing. It was now viewed as a trance or altered state of awareness that was psychic in nature. In other words, it is a manifestation or expression of a mysterious, pulsating energy field that emotionally connects two or more individuals.

James Braid, in 1844, coined the term hypnosis after he experienced this energy field (a trance) in the company of two friends. Braid had been influenced by the Far Eastern mystical trance practices that I described in chapter six. He named hypnosis for *Hypnos*, the sleep god of ancient mythology who was the son of *Nyx* (night) and brother of *Thanatos* (death). At his Nancy school, Emile Coue labeled this trance pattern autosuggestion. That is, we must think or imagine properly and develop our receptivity to this process in order to acquire the results we want. Can an individual transform talk into action? Can we create a psychic condition in which an individual is susceptible to suggestion? Questions such as these mark the beginnings of modern day psychotherapy.

Hypnotic treatments became a dramatic, enticing offer of transformation that in reality was little different than the rituals and methods employed during the Golden Age of Greece. The common theme was love-seeking, broken romances and hope for the future. The common method was the trance. Aspects of Gall's phrenology, such as manipulation of the scalp, a technique employed by Braid, could produce hypnotized subjects sinking to their knees in prayer. Hypnotic treatments work best when the hypnotist or therapist that initiates the trance has the confidence that their methods will be effective. Therapeutic practitioners must be connected to their own emotional brain energy patterns and have acquired the skills to use this art form that releases tension and elevates energy patterns. It is like a talent for music or poetry and cannot be conducted with an intellectual technique-oriented approach. Remember my teacher, Dr. Peter Sifneos? He tried to use this hypnotic technique because it worked so well for one of his colleagues who had attained sensational results in treating certain patients. It could not work for him because he had limited access to his own emotional expression and was more focused on his distant, scientific manner of relating.

In hypnosis and other related states, such as meditation and relaxation training, the participant acquires the skill to forget her or his individual self and surrender to another voice or energy, usually that of the hypnotist. The I or Me fade into a nothingness in which the experiencer comes in contact with a powerful force within the self that is still and open to change. In this hypnotic state there is a paradox. By giving up rational control of themselves, individuals rise to another level of awareness that is invigorating and transformative, often increasing their own personal strength of mind. Some behavioral scientists term this an altered state. Still others call it dissociation, that is, a person is split off or dissociated from her or his normal memory and awareness. Another conceptualization theorizes that it is merely role-playing.

Whatever the rationale may be, when in a trance or hypnotic state, we can experience creative and emotional changes such as reduction in pain and assume the ability to take on many roles, just as if we had become a child again. We can function with inconsistencies in logic such as, "She/he is married to someone else, but really loves me and is really married to me."

The capacity to fantasize is the most important ingredient required to activate this process. I remember my dad carrying me in his arms just before bedtime out to the tall grandfather clock in the front parlor. He would tell me to listen to the tick and tock of the clock and soon the sandman would come out of the clock to put me to sleep. My father's somnolent voice mingled with the soothing tones of the clock as gradually the tick tock sound overtook my consciousness. My awareness faded into a sleeping forgetfulness.

Trance states have been happening since the beginning of man. In fact, the Greek term *ate*, a love surging impulse, implies a hypnotic process in the altering of consciousness. Groups of specialists have created a role or occupation and thus attempted to bestow upon themselves a recognizable legitimacy by acting as if they know something special and mysterious. They could be best described as mediums or conduits for inducing changes and attitudes in people. Most of the modern therapies teach or instruct patients/clients in methods of relaxation to reduce anxiety and stress. Self-regulating, self-hypnotic (autogenic) training has been recognized for over one hundred years as a method for the individual to release his/her own tension. Another self-regulating technique, which has been around for thousands of years, is natural yogic breathing exercises.

The common thread of all these experiences is that if we can manifest and activate our natural capacity to engage our emotional brain, we are available to receive hypnotic energy from another person(s) that develops in us creative energy, thoughts, plans and zest for the future.

WILLIAM JAMES, THE FATHER OF AMERICAN PSYCHOLOGY: TRANCE AND ALTERED STATES

William James (1842–1910 AD) is considered the founder of American psychology. He established the first American psychological laboratory in 1874 and published a two volume text in 1890, twelve years after he agreed to write it. After completing this great work, he was reputed to state that there is no such thing as a pure science of psychology. Since he was so interested in inner psychic states of awareness, psychic healing and clairvoyance, he was not recognized by his more scientifically-oriented peers. James disagreed vehemently on many mystical and scientific issues with Wilhelm Wundt (1832–1920 AD), the German empirically oriented psychologist who has been given credit for establishing psychology as a science.

In the 1880s James wrote extensively about the emotions, memory and multiple states of consciousness. He was quite transparent as he related his personal life experiences in his scientific writings. He described his depression, wishes and desires, one of which was to stay in bed all day. It seems James was subjected to the intense psychic states of pain and inner psychic awareness that all mystics experience. His father, Henry, was a hound of heaven and had become a follower of the mystical, scientific, energetic approach of Emmanuel Swedenborg. These experiences created in William strong desires to investigate the mysterious psychological nuances and complexities of life, including situations when one part of the self is unable to bring into consciousness events that have split off from the self's core personality. He termed this inability to recall memories, *dissociative behavior*. In modern terminology we sometimes refer to this as split off ego states. This situation happens frequently in intense emotional situations, most frequently in matters of love.

Just around the time Freud was publishing his *Interpretation of Dreams*, James published his *Varieties of Religious Experiences*. This work focuses on the self-healing capacity of an individual in order to experience the good things of living. Beneath our human suffering is our desire for a connection to contact and become transformed by transient, emotionally-elevating, mystical states. We cannot read about this kind of awareness and knowledge, we must directly experience these mystical trance states, very much as we have to feel and experience love.

FREUD, JUNG AND SABINA SPIELREIN

In the early twentieth century, at the same time that leading experts, such as Pierre Janet, had come to America to discuss hypnotic healing methods with William James and other experts, Sigmund Freud arrived in the summer of 1909 to give his psychoanalytic lectures at Clark University in Worcester, Massachusetts. On the boat trip, he and his budding young associate, Carl Jung, experienced a falling out. Apparently in 1906, Jung sought Freud's advice about his romantic attraction to Sabina Spielrein, his first patient at the Burghölzli hospital in 1905. He was thirty. Sabina was in her late teens. These almost daily sessions that continued for four years were passionately intense and resplendent with creative displays of love and reflection. They considerably influenced Jung's personality formulations concerning the nature of the mind. Sabina and Jung's formal relationship ended about the time of Freud and Jung's boat trip to America.

I am sure the discussion between Freud and Jung concerning Sabina, and Freud's fainting on the boat trip stirred up intense emotional reactions in both men. Freud was tuning into the sexual attraction between Jung and Sabina. Jung was searching for approaches to elevate these troublesome, arousing feelings and soon thereafter began his quest into the Eastern world's inner psychic science healing methods. Had not the *Tibetan Book of the Dead* already described a man's hatred for his father, what Freud was calling the Oedipus complex? Freud was a scientifically-oriented positivist and labeled these religious conjectures as child-like omnipotent fantasies. He himself had been previously addicted to cocaine and even had recommended it as a medical treatment. His goal was now to innovate a biological model for the science of the mind with his newly developed psychoanalytic techniques. Such an interesting Freud, Jung, and Sabina triangle with all its mystery and intrigue!

Sabina herself was very intelligent and innovative. She eventually became a psychoanalyst and formulated views that became part of psychoanalytic practices. In 1909 she had requested a meeting with Freud. He declined, due to her relationship with Jung. They did meet in 1911 after Freud and Jung broke up. Freud was enthralled with her spunky manner of relating and her creative capacity to illuminate and expand his theoretical treatment approaches. Sabina published and presented her own original methods of treatment in the emerging field of child psychology. Her innovative contributions made a considerable impact on subsequent generations of psychoanalysts. Unhappily, she lived a stormy personal life, encountering many difficulties.

PSYCHOTHERAPEUTIC FORMULATIONS

Mental health treatment was expanding and becoming more popular in America in the early twentieth century. Dr. Joseph Pratt, a pioneer physician at Tufts Medical School, instituted group therapy sessions for his patients that were conducted by religious practitioners at their churches, such as the Episcopal Emmanuel Church and Roman Catholic Mission Church. Matters of love, relationships, and coping with psychosomatic symptoms were the usual topics for discussion. Effective healing outcome testimonials were in the thousands.

World War I combat encounters resulted in many psychological causalities. Mental health treatments were needed. Group therapy approaches became an efficient model for helping veterans in emotional distress. The talking cure and emotional expression and abreaction with their spazzing components were considered a new treatment modality. Psychoanalysis replaced the hypnotic trance state as the favored method of treatment. These providers had medical degrees and considered themselves to be extremely knowledgeable. In fact, they had a diagnosis for everyone's behavior. They developed a reputation for naming, but not taming, a problem. The patient's resistance was considered the roadblock to a successful outcome. It was said psychoanalysis could go on forever.

A modified, revised version of this psychoanalytic approach achieved a better result. An individual's capacities to observe her or himself as well as exploring defense mechanisms, were considered to be very important factors for a successful therapeutic outcome. Among psychotherapists, methodologies and techniques continue to be argued. Even today groups of therapists form associations and societies to further their own models of therapy, often to the exclusion of other more effective methods for treating a problem that a patient presents.

I contend that there is a trance pattern operating in these groups much in the same manner as William James theorized that emotional states heavily influence one's rational thinking. These groups of professionals can be likened to the many religious sects that splintered off from their mainstream group, all claiming to have a rational reason for their approach and the ability to facilitate change. What they do not realize is that they are employing trance-like hypnotic phenomena. The rational content usually consists of metaphors that are secondary to the emotional, brain-driven energy that is arising and being exchanged among the participants.

THE DODO BIRD VERDICT AND PSYCHOTHERAPY

Many therapists of today forget the conclusions of the research findings of Saul Rosenzweig written in 1936 concerning the Dodo Bird Verdict. This analogy refers to the story in *Alice in Wonderland* in which a number of birds and other animals were all soaking wet and agitated. The dodo bird suggested that they run a race in a circle to see who could dry the fastest. Many of the creatures, however, ran in their own unique ways in a chaotic fashion. After thirty minutes or so of running, all were dry and the dodo bird declared the race was over. All the participants crowded around the dodo bird and wanted to know who had won. After much reflection the dodo bird stated, "Everybody has won. All must have prizes."

Alice was selected by the dodo bird to provide the prizes. She pulled out of her pocket a box of fruited candies called comfits and gave one to each of the participants. The Rosenzweig formulation concludes that the relationship with the therapist is more important than the technique. The late personality theorist and therapist, Raymond Corsini, expanded on this formulation and stated that a successful therapist utilizes a theory and employs techniques that are reflective of his or her own personality.

I contend that the trance-like healing pattern between the therapist and patient is the key component of an effective psychotherapeutic healing process. The famous behavior therapy researcher, W. Horsley Gantt, called it the effect of person. The art form of listening in order to help people is very necessary. Psychotherapists–healers must be able to collaborate, listen and communicate in their patient's language and culture and, like the oracles of old, be optimistic about the future. Their techniques are frequently secondary to their capacity to be present-centered, to listen and provide the proper climate and feedback to their patients. This encourages them to access their own creative inner resources to resolve their issues, and to become competent and take charge of their lives. As we have discussed in our many cases, the therapist is simply an instrument and humble conduit for this restorative and balancing life force-generated energy, especially in regard to matters of love.

10.

LOVE RELATED PROBLEMS AND SOLUTIONS

LOVE SEARCHING

Dr. Julia was a young, attractive, and very intelligent intern at our clinic. She had acquired extensive intellectual knowledge at her university. Acquiring information, collecting data, and doing research is different when your academic knowledge can interfere and become bondage in your interactions with some patients. Her training program in psychology, however, had not emotionally prepared her for what she was experiencing with her patient, Clement Cranston, who had sought counseling because his wife thought he was too flighty and not spending enough time with her. Catherine Cranston felt he was not a good husband because he went out to a night club with his buddies one night a week. This was the third marriage for both. He had children by his first marriage, she had no children and was hoping to settle down and have one with Mr. Cranston.

Clement really did not want to change a lot. He wanted to do something, but wasn't sure what he wanted to do in terms of relationships. Dr. Julia, moreover, felt he was coming on to her. He was looking at her in a piercing manner with gawking, staring eyes. He sometimes spoke to her softly in a seductive tone. At times, Dr. Julia felt that he saw their meetings as a date.

As the seminar leader, I suggested that she arrange for Mr. Cranston to meet with the seminar. The eight participants included four women, three men, and me. I interviewed Mr. Cranston. Initially, he spent most of the time gawking at an attractive female intern who was present in the group. I called his attention to his behavior. Mr. Cranston acknowledged his behavior and attraction. I then asked him if he would leave his wife for another, more attractive, person.

"Hell yes," was his response.

Mr. Cranston did not, however, acknowledge what had been happening in Dr. Julia's office. He did admit to his constant craving and love-seeking desires. I gently informed him that he had *kundalitis*, that incessant love sickness that I described in great detail during my navy days. Whatever he was attracted to aroused and excited him on many planes, both physically and psychically. It is a compulsion that has its biological origins in the base brain. If he was serious about working on his marriage, he would need to acquire focusing and containing techniques that would enable him to enjoy his present relationship and control his wandering eyes and agitated mind.

Dr. Julia felt somewhat better after the seminar meeting. She acknowledged her jealousy, confusion and anger, especially about how Mr. Cranston's love searching madness induced him to focus on a new, attractive woman, completely ignoring her. With this insight into his love searching behavior, Dr. Julia was able to move forward in confronting and containing Mr. Cranston's incessant love searching inclinations. Focusing and improving his relationship with his wife became the goal of the treatment.

RUSTY'S LOVE SICKNESS.

Rusty was possessed by lovesickness in a different fashion. His dad had played around and mom had divorced him. He was his mom's love child. There was something special between him and her. He had two younger brothers. They didn't mean much to him or his mother.

Rusty had been rejected in his love quests a number of times. He met and married Peggy on the rebound. They knew each other from high school. Peggy was easy-going and not the jealous type. She seemed to have a good beat on him. People wondered why she was so tolerant of his constant searches for new loves. He loved to share his romantic stories with his mother. Peggy didn't mind, she had her own mom to talk to. Rusty worked; she stayed at home with their young son. They were somewhat happy until she had their second son. It was just like what had happened to Rusty when his mother had had his brother, a second son. Rusty was upset. Now with Peggy betraying him the way his mother had, he stayed at home lying in a stupor on his bed complaining that he was quite ill and had no energy. It was as if he had post-partum depression. Peggy even said he had the "baby blues." She telephoned me and asked what she should do since Rusty did not want to go to work. A spontaneous, creative infusion of energy, similar to that described by the Greek term *menos*, surged into my awareness and, without thinking, I told her to place the new baby boy beside him in bed and lay there with them. Rusty jumped out of bed, got dressed, and went to work. The next day in my office he informed me that I "sucked" as a therapist. He told me that I did not understand him. He was back in his routine in about a week.

About a year later, Rusty was back in the office. He wanted to leave Peggy and their family, like his Dad had left his mom and his brothers. His old girlfriend, Sally, had invited him to go out and get back together. Peggy did not seem to be extremely upset, but was rather resigned, although she did insist that he come and talk with me.

Again, I immediately reacted in a transparent, somewhat playful manner. I spoke to Rusty as we fellow navy medics would tease each other.

"Be a jerk, go out with her again, and she will send you on your way as she did before."

He looked at me with a perplexed face and left the session stymied by my comments. In about a month's time we met again. Rusty asked, "What evidence did you have to tell me that she would break up with me again?"

"Did she?" I asked.

"Yes, and I never want to see you again in my life. You know more about me than I do."

That "you" is the therapist dramatizing the future like the ancient Greek oracles and Roman sibyls. They can be more effective if they are willing to take a risk and engage at more than a rational level with their patients, particularly when it comes to matters of love.

Rusty had that love-seeking and love searching sickness called *kundalitis*. The entire world was about him and that which he felt attracted to. Being angry at me kept his mad love searching self in check and activated his thinking self. When his love searching behavior resurfaced, the image of his therapist presented itself and this put a damper on his love searching madness and contained his behavior. Rusty views me as someone who does not understand his needs. He is correct. In his emotional brain driven mind he should be able to have all of his girlfriends. To him, I am the irrational one. In a seven-year follow-up, Rusty was still with Peggy and the father of their third child

DOUBLE DATE

The story of Joyce began with her coming into therapy to discuss whether she should get back together with her husband, Vincent. She had met him in college and they married soon after graduation. They had been married for three years when that divine love searching madness the ancient Greeks called *ate* took over their life and that of another couple, Cindy and Ted. After double dating a few times, they decided to swap partners. Things went well until about six months into the relationship experiment when Cindy announced to Vincent that she no longer wanted to be with him. Joyce and Ted were enjoying their relationship, but Joyce felt bad for leaving Vincent.

"I am married to Vincent," Joyce would declare, "but I don't know what to do." She had repeated calls from Vincent, pleading with her to come back.

"It was stupid, crazy and wrong for us to do this," he would whine.

We discussed this issue for a year and decided together that Joyce would make a choice within the next two months. Instead, Mother Nature made the decision for her. She was pregnant with Ted's child. Vincent's interest in reconciling evaporated.

A NATURAL SOLUTION

Babies and pregnancy are major issues in any relationship, particularly in young adult lives. George and Barbara came to see me to work out a marital issue. They both had previously been in long-term relationships that did not work out. They were in their mid-thirties when they were blessed with a son. Barbara reacted with a postpartum depression. She psychically regressed to an earlier period in her life when she was with her true love, Alex, and in her mind thought of him as the father of her baby. George had known all about Alex, and Barbara's fondness for him. He tried to persuade Barbara that he was the father of this child and not Alex. She would hear nothing of it. She persisted in her fantasy, even to the point of arranging a christening with only herself and her own friends present. I requested that the christening be postponed for a few months while we dealt with Barbara's emotional flooding, so that her symptoms, particularly her agitation, would have time to recede. During our session Barbara tearfully lamented

"I really don't want anything to do with you, George. Our relationship is a joke. You know I still really love Alex and not you, George."

Now George was a mature and reflective man. He loved Barbara and wanted the best for her. He was warm, caring and constantly reiterated that he was the father of the child.

Time plays a factor in these transient states of confusion and dissociation. We gradually worked out a satisfactory date for the christening. Barbara let George invite his family and friends. A joyful celebration took place and Barbara seemed to be pleased.

A few weeks later I received a phone call from George. "Barbara is back to her old self. Our family is fine. We are all fine. Barbara is pregnant." Reality set in and Mother Nature solved their problem.

THE POOR SOUL

The poor soul has been meeting with me for several years. He would very much like to find a girl friend, settle down and marry, but cannot claim the attributes that women are drawn to. He speaks in a monotonous manner, is so boring, dull and methodical, that women do not find him attractive or appealing. Instead of succumbing to the maddening energy of Eros, he remains stalled in the ivory tower of his rational brain.

The Soul was quite athletic in his younger day and keeps himself in shape by going to the gym. He loves to chat with some of the regular gym-goers, but they find his conversations boring since he is always seeking information. Part of his regular entertainment is to surf dating web sites. He even has purchased many self-help manuals on dating tips, but is hampered and often upset that their techniques are not logical and do not seem to work for him. His attention to detail is so strong that he very much would like to know the exact time when he would ejaculate during sexual activity. Even the holy ladies who work at this profession have suggested that he not return to their consulting rooms.

I have encouraged him to attend cultural events so that he can relate to people who have similar interests. The Soul's ritualistic behavior patterns have prevented him from surrendering his obsessive, private peccadilloes and reacting to people at a meaningful emotional level. It bothered him most severely when he was young. Now he is learning to accept himself as he is, but not without hope of finding a relationship sometime in the future.

UNRESOLVED RESOLUTIONS OF EARLY CHILDHOOD SEXUAL STIMULATION

There is a psychic aspect of our personality patterns in which we as individuals relate to the world as if everything is only about Me. This is an old reptilian brain-driven energy field that is referred to as the *grandiose self*. In its intense expression it is mania. The young child initially relates to his parents as an extension of that Me, that perfectly adorable, god-like love child. That infectious, emotional-brain-generated joyful, loving smile that this godlike, energetic, zestful product of nature emits, signals the beginning of brand new adventures. The child rewards its caretakers who provide nourishment and change its diaper with gratitude in the form of cuddliness and closeness and at other times with strong emotional displays of intense rage reactions. In this state of self-centered awareness the child views everything that is happening in relation to its self so that it is just about Me, much in the same manner that Thrush, my cat, related to the world with the mantra, "Meow, Me now."

The child's first major confrontation with psychobiology relates to mom and dad's sexual activity. A child's experience is forever altered when she/he discovers that she/he is not welcome to participate in this event. Cultures have been aware for centuries that babies frequently cry when this old brain, self-focused, emotional energy pattern is being expressed. Freud himself wrote a treatise about a young Russian prince who developed nightmares and terrors of wolves after viewing his parents' sexual engagement. According to my very dynamic teacher, Dr. Morris Adler, the young lad gets over this experience by identifying with his father as he modifies his original anger and rage into positive idealistic energy. This happens because he can't do it. He cannot swing the bat. His hormones don't kick in until adolescence when he is biologically capable of "playing the game."

KJ could not let go of the primal scene. He came into the world shortly after the family's first child did not want to. She had died during birth. KJ was a loving, healthy baby. His dad adored him. His mother worshipped him. A few years later a sister came along. It was hard for KJ to share his parents' affection that had always been for him alone. He reacted to her arrival by competing with his sister and pretending that he was both a boy and a girl. Later in life, he styled himself after Orlando, the unisex character in Virginia Wolff's novel.

KJ and I began our therapeutic sessions shortly after his mother passed away at the age of sixty. He was twenty-four. After several sessions mourning her loss he revealed a major incident that happened when he was about five years old and had been bothering him throughout most of his life. One rainy Sunday afternoon while he was playing games with his sister, he heard roars of thunder and flashes of lightning and ran into his parents' bedroom seeking comfort. Little did he know that he was walking in on the primal scene. KJ felt stunned and overwhelmed, so excited, angry, jealous and thirsty. Dad told him to "scram." He stood still waiting for his mother to beckon him to her. He was shocked that there was no invitation from her for him to join them in the game. They did not want him. They did not need him, this perfect one. He was frozen in time. He did not know what to do. Did they have any empathy or understanding of his situation? No. Did they really love him? No. He whined his song of anger. They ignored him as his dada continued his activity, thrusting and thumping. He isn't sure, but thinks his father was also cursing him. They made lots of noises and wild laughter. He so wanted to be made part of this. He slammed the door as he ran out of the room, sitting at the threshold listening to the musical sounds and thunderous noise of the bed rattling in his distraught and excited ears. He began consoling and soothing himself by playing with his own joy toy.

A few days later as the events of that Sunday afternoon's primal scene were intruding into his consciousness he struck his sister on the head with a miniature baseball bat his parents had given him for his birthday. He thought he had killed her right there. That evening she began to have seizures and thus began a slow process of deterioration and eventual death three years later. KJ began to relive what happened on that thunder and lightning filled Sunday afternoon. His angry, exciting and confusing reaction influenced how he related to the world for most of his life. He also began to develop a perfect devotion to his mom as he tried to please her in every manner. He felt intensely angry and competitive with his father for mom's attention. During his middle school years he took martial arts classes and voice lessons so he could be a skillful and admired performer. Family matters were rather routine until at the age of eleven mom shockingly discovered that dad had been carrying on for years with a co-worker. It was again on another rainy Sunday afternoon that mom and dad had a huge confrontation over his extramarital activity. Dad left the house in a rage. He drove his car into a tree and went to God.

Now the pre-adolescent KJ was left at home with mom and began to flourish. This prince took over many chores in the household as mom went to work. The entitled young boy was determined not to betray his mother. He began, however, to demonstrate rages of his own, not unlike his dad. He could also experience strong bouts of sadness and depression. During his high school years his male peers would tease him about his haughtiness. He abhorred the many male adolescent rituals and cliques. He wanted to be his own person

Following high school graduation, KJ enrolled in a music school to study voice and piano. On one of the school's excursions to Paris he met up with some socialites in the music scene. They took a fancy to him. He began to observe that everyone wanted to "play" with him and he began to feel quite anxious at the thought of being physically close with anyone. He chose not to return home with his school group. He loved Paris. He felt like he was a star. He developed a penchant for having a sponsor to pay his bills and would express his displeasure if matters were not to his liking. His attitude toward anyone interested in him was, "Just look. Do not touch".

The reoccurring images of that rainy Sunday afternoon sexual activity never really left his awareness. In his mind there was no rational solution, just a replay of that experience, which in psychological terms is called "the approach–avoidance phenomenon." Many people experience this in matters of love and connection. In KJ's situation, the primal scene of the past generated too much anxiety and impaired his own ability to relate and love. He could not tolerate physical sexual contact, hampered by the burden of his reaction to his parents' intimacy and their treatment of him. Most individuals forget or repress this experience, pursuing relationships. This arrested developmental resolution, that is, KJ's inability to separate himself from his mother and father, continued to dominate his patterns of relating and transacting.

Time and biology wait for no man. KJ's mom remained back home alone, getting along in years and becoming frail. Mom was no longer the voluptuous lady, the image that KJ's brain had planted in his psyche and nurtured for all those years. She was ill and dying and asked him to come home. It was so difficult to watch her leaving the world. His heart felt all her pain and sorrow. He felt guilty for not spending more time with her. She died a few weeks later. KJ left home again to complete his musical studies in another city. His good luck and musical skills continued to work for him. He became very suspicious and anxious at the thought of engaging or gratifying any of his sponsors who had a wild physical attraction to him.

To console himself during all these years he played his own music on his tom-tom. (He would masturbate.) In his self-consoling quietude, he could relive his early boyhood perfection and have life on his terms. In his new surroundings he was able to obtain a job as a caretaker for a wealthy family. He imagined himself as a member of this well-to-do family and carried on as if it was so. He acted quite regally with his fellow students. They frequently came up against his arrogant attitude that they were not good enough for him. He acted haughtily and condescendingly, but in his heart and inner self he longed to be close to someone who could share love with him. He continued to reap the benefits of his luck and charm when he obtained the position of lead soloist at a well-endowed church in the city. He adored the adulation. He had become a star, albeit a frightened one.

"Is there someone out there my own age that can understand me, be my friend?" KJ wondered to himself. There seemed to be many gentle loving faces in the congregation. As he scanned the church from high on his perch in the choir loft, he spotted the calm gentle face of a lad his own age. He was seated with an attractive young lady who had similar facial features. KJ became aroused and overwhelmed. His heart began to beat rapidly; his breath and pulse accelerated. "There is something about this guy. Can I make a friend with whom I can talk? Can I meet the brother that I always wanted? Can I find some real comfort in this life? Will he introduce me to his sister?" Hope springs eternal. KJ fantasized something wonderful happening to enrich his life and find the love that he always had been seeking.

ROGER AND TONY

Roger's mom was a straight-laced Yankee lady. She was a faithful wife and dutiful mother. Roger was the oldest in a family of three, a well-developed, good-looking athlete. He was somewhat shy, but had a few friends. He just had one vice.

He loved holy pictures (girly magazines). Being a curious and excitable lad at sixteen he loved to view the beautiful ladies and express his love through "manual manipulation." One day his mom discovered him engaging in his "prayerful worshipping state." She felt betrayed and enraged.

"How could you do this to me?" she screamed, furiously jealous.

Roger was shocked, confused and compliant. She did not want him to share his life with other women. He pleased her and took up playing with boys.

A few years after college, while working out at the gym, Roger met Tony, a man his own age. They bonded and interacted at many levels. Roger seemed to be content, enjoying sporting events and playing boy ball. Tony had another agenda. He was also in love with his college girlfriend. He did not hide his amorous relationship with Linda from Roger. The closer they felt toward each other, the more distraught Roger became in having to share Tony.

Roger's dad had many women friends, which his mother would not tolerate. This resulted in divorce. Roger then became his mother's confidante. Roger still related to his dad and considered him to be a great father, albeit a distant one. Roger was very close to his mom, but did not want to share his love life with her due to her intrusive behavior during his teenage years.

Matters came to a head when Tony asked Roger to be the best man at his wedding. Roger would hear nothing of it. He felt betrayed and demanded that Tony choose him or Linda. Tony chose Linda. Roger went off on a long vacation and refused to have anything more to do with Tony. He joined a different gym and tried to make a new life, but all those other guys did not have the charm and affection that Tony had shared with him. He was heartbroken. After about a year Tony started to beg Roger to get back together.

"I know it is strange for you and you think you were

dumped, but you dumped me. I am miserable. I love my wife, but I love you too."

"Fuck you," was Roger's reply. "You made your choice."

Soon Roger went into a deep depression and began consulting with me. His professional work was rewarding, but in the realm of his social life he felt lonely and isolated. He went through his daily routines, but felt a paralyzing emptiness. He was depressed.

Within a few months, Roger and Tony decided to get together to try to resolve the wild madness for each other that they each kept experiencing despite being apart for a long time. It was not only the sexual relationship, but also the intense psychic love they had for each other, a mad psychophysical closeness that they felt, but could not express with words. Despite this reunion, they could not resolve their lifestyle issues. Roger still refused to participate in Tony's life with Linda. He still felt hurt and chose to move to a different city. He wanted to get away from this love madness and start over. Time will tell. The mixing of heartbeats and an authentic psychic connection is difficult to let go of and even harder to attempt to replace.

THE RIGHT TO LOVE

Ron's mom also tortured him emotionally. She was lonely and in his youth wanted him to be her companion for life. He revolted and became a marine, a fighter, but more than anything else, he wanted to be a lover. He did not have much luck until he ran into Kelly. They did nice things together, drank beer, smoked pot, and did a few other substances. They were one of the many couples that made the trip to Woodstock. This closeness to Kelly drove Ron mad as the alluring image of his mother began to intrude into their relationship. Ron became controlling, assaultive and possessive. He wanted to supervise Kelly's every move. She could not take his badgering and importunate behavior, left him and took out a restraining order. This has been going on for over twenty years. He kept pursuing her.

"She is the only one I could really feel love for."

Ron spent most of his money on attorney's fees, attempting to remove the restraining order. In the meantime his mother had passed away. He did not seem to give this much attention. He also began doing martial arts and attending yoga classes. He learned how to restrain and contain his very assertive, argumentative, assaultive behavior.

With a little help from me, he argued before the judge in court that he had "a right to love." That is, to express his love searching emotions. He contended that this restraining order was prohibiting him from exercising his constitutional right to life, loving and the pursuit of his personal happiness. Such an interesting view, thought I.

A date was set to go before the judge. To the surprise of Ron, a haggard, wrinkled old lady appeared in the courtroom. He was in a rage.

"This is not the woman I loved. She is an imposter!"

With support from our group meetings he began to acknowledge he had been pursuing a dream. His image of his perfect love of twenty plus years ago was no more than a figment of his imagination, a ghost of his past. He had been deceived by time and nature.

"This new, old woman reminds you of your own mother," said I.

"Ya, I have all her aches and pains to prove it," said Ron. "What I need is a vacation from you, her, and everyone else. I am on my own with all this pain and madness. Maybe I can let go and really love someone again."

LOVE, MADNESS, SEX AND VIOLENCE

D anny was six-feet-tall, a well-built, athletic ex-marine who I met when he was in his late twenties. His short-cropped hair and the U.S. Marine Corps' tattoo on his left forearm were his signals to the world that he still felt strongly connected to the battlefield deep in the jungles of Vietnam. A mysterious smirk would come over Danny when discussing his war experiences. We initially met in a communications group that I was conducting for combat veterans.

Danny lived life from a different perspective. He was not one to feel shame and boasted about the pleasure he felt when parading his nude body around in the gym locker room. He actually commented in a very matter-of-fact manner that Michelangelo's sculpture of David was his ideal image of the real warrior. He did point out, however, that David's dick should have been fully erect as he was poised to let go his slingshot at the giant, Goliath. Danny related particularly to the part of the story when David took Goliath's own sword to further mutilate him, for Danny had a strong attraction to knives, guns, sling shots—any kind of weapon. He made no excuse for his intense, erotic arousal and excitement while using these instruments and assumed that everyone else secretly felt the same as he did. In combat he had killed a young teenage boy. He cut off his penis. He said that he felt real good doing it. He even ejaculated during the process. He merged with him physically and psychically in a psychotic fashion. He took the boy's picture from his identification tag and religiously carried it in his wallet. He felt a oneness with this boy. He was also very sad and guilty about what he did.

"I can't help it. I try to control myself. The rush is maddening."

In contrast to this bizarre behavior, he was extremely verbal and articulate and over the years became a training patient. He would meet with a group of medical students and present to them his symptoms of posttraumatic stress disorder. He would answer their questions and explain his lifestyle to them, as well as instructing them on the nature of war trauma and his personal adjustment. He had many therapists over the years and in a sense was a favorite patient because of both the charm and the challenge he presented. They each had their evidenced-based techniques in attempting to "cure" him. His intelligence level and verbal skills made him an interesting and engaging patient. I took over coordinating his treatment at the time when a well-meaning, behaviorally-oriented team was attempting to treat him for early childhood trauma. This group of therapists uncovered an incident in which a YMCA worker sexually fondled him. Danny became so enraged when this memory was uncovered that he wanted to kill the YMCA worker.

The therapists were so overwhelmed by the intensity of his reaction and possible homicidal potential that they discontinued his treatment and referred him to me. My role in our clinic over the years was to patch up difficult issues and incidents that occurred in patients' psychotherapy. Danny and I were no strangers and had very good rapport from our previous group contact.

Danny had also taken classes in hypnosis with other therapists and exhibited a calm, tranquil side in his personality patterns. I used this interest to help him reduce his arousal level, which was one of his major problems. We began a program of hypnotic breathing and relaxation for neutralizing this intensely stimulating and emotionally flooding event. I told him to forget and let go of this madness of a long ago event and to become present-centered and focus on his wife and family. Danny realized that he had many other issues to deal with rather than this early childhood sexual encounter.

During one of his other treatment groups, conducted by a different therapist, he began crying wildly when told that another patient had just had a heart attack and died. He was uncontrollable in his grief and his therapists requested that he meet with me for an emergency consultation. During our session my intuition was that there was something else troubling him and I expressed that to him. He tearfully told me that his wife had scratched him badly the previous night. Without any warning he pulled up his shirt and displayed multiple cuts and deep, oozing, scratches. This grown, ex-marine was crying like a little boy. I asked him, "What did you do to deserve this?"

He then confessed that he was "out on the town last night and up to no good."

"You're lucky that is all she did," I stated.

Danny's crying slowly changed to soft sobbing. With further tension release and dialogue he composed himself and felt comforted. His wife's physical attack was an attempt on her part to challenge his lifestyle and behavior. Danny eventually returned to his group and was grateful for our brief session.

About a year later, against my advice, Danny went on an excursion to Central America for a recreational hunting trip. Another friend had lived there the previous winter and invited him to accompany him on this trip. He returned home after a few weeks and tearfully reported that he had knifed and killed a man while he was on his trip. It seems the person tried to attack and rob him. Danny welcomed this attempted assault. It brought him back to the battlefield in Vietnam. He experienced the same adrenaline rush in killing this thug who was wanted by the law. No government criminal charges were pressed. In a sense, Danny viewed himself as a hero. As part of their training experience my medical students interviewed Danny. They reacted with shock and horror as they heard him describe this gruesome tale. It was too difficult for them to process their own emotional reactions to what they had just experienced. I spent several sessions teaching the students the circle breath exercise to release their tensions and emotional reactions and describing the mindset and symptoms of a warrior who daily experienced wild surges of sexual and aggressive energy.

Danny also had a great love for many kinds of substances that would connect him to the divine-like state of eros. He had become addicted to painkillers as a result of a physical injury he had received in combat. He frequently would toy with drug dealers who provided him with bad quality drugs by taking them by surprise at knifepoint. He reported that he felt as if he was back in the jungle on a mission in the war. His heart beat rapidly as his bodily sensations became so excitable that he experienced full sexual arousal with a very powerful stiff phallus guiding his activity. He felt invincible. He was not afraid of anything, including death. He confronted two dealers and threatened them with cutting off their genitals. He tortured them with knives and guns and made them plead for their lives.

"In that state, I can make them blow me, suck themselves or any other activity I so desire. I am the grand master. I am god."

He continued his torture. He took all their money and burned it. He told them he would kill them next time if they sold him low quality drugs. They pleaded with him. He let them go. Danny had been through this event many times. He loved to be excited and to feel the kill and the accompanying sexual thrill. It is a primal re-creation of the excitement of battle.

Back home his wife awaited his arrival. The baby had gone to sleep and his wife was feeling very lonely. Danny came home tired, exhausted and somewhat exhilarated. He looked at her. She was beautiful. He had a hard time dealing with her loving sensual expression and her wish to engage. Interacting with her brought back the encounter he had just experienced with the two drug dealers he had confronted. He felt love and excitement for her. He was afraid if he did something he might try to kill her. She started to swear at him and called him a "pussy". She teased him and ridiculed him for being out with the boys. Her anger intensified into a boiling rage as he became numb and avoided her. He thought to himself, "What's going on with me? I'm impotent. I have no sexual energy."

She continued her vituperative, verbal assaults and slapped him on the face as she tormented him about his ineffective sexual prowess. He started to examine his thoughts. He thought if he fucked her he would kill her. He was frozen. He did not understand. Neither did she. They had a stormy fight. He left. She cried, "Why, why, why?"

He arrived at my office and reported he had a headache. He began to experience his inner psychic despair and agitation. I initiated a breathing exercise that helped him compose himself and focus on what he had been experiencing. He continued to express himself and in a soft crying voice related his tales of horror and mayhem. Quiet listening while he talked, healed and soothed his psyche as he continued to pause and engage in a connecting, centering breathing exercise. He yearned to reestablish reality, to be able to resume his normal activities. A soft tap on the chest generated a non-intrusive grounding and reconnection to his psychic and physical self. Then Danny began to sob as he reported that he felt dead as the intensity of the flashbacks to his battle scenes continued to intrude on his consciousness—his dead friends, the mayhem, the futility, the nothingness. After his tension was released Danny's breathing became normal as he eventually connected to a calmed inner self. He feels love. He is at peace. I ask him if there is more to life than repeating these violent cycles of death, rage and love.

"Not really," says he. "There are so many people that I carry around with me. I owe them my life. I get to release my madness with you. You have taught me to love and respect my body, but I still want to die."

"It is a psychic death," I tell him.

"Ya."

"You have a wife and son to live for. Go do it."

"Ya. Give me a hug."

"See you next week."

Danny went home. His wife was still waiting to love. He experienced a powerful physical and psychic connection with her. They talked. All was well. It had been three days of mad living. The gates of love open. What is Danny about? What is up with all these multiple manifestations of energy fields of love, sexuality, aggression and violence? I will share my views in the next chapter.

11.

PSEUDOSEXUAL DARK ENERGY PATTERNS

A HOLLYWOOD STORY: DARK ENERGY

Can you remember the movie *Good Will Hunting* and the scene when Will (Matt Damon) was being treated by his psychologist, Sean Maguire (Robin Williams)? Their meeting flows into a surging, non-verbal, tumultuous, emotionally-flooding situation as Will begins reliving his past. Sean tells Will several times that it is not his fault. Will agrees and then becomes silent as that underlying, dark, rippling energy begins to subtly seep into his awareness. Sean speaks, "It's not your fault." Will's eyes begin to close. Sean moves physically closer to Will and speaks in a hypnotic, commanding tone, "It's not your fault." Will begins feeling this dark energy overtaking him and yells, "Don't fuck with me, Sean. Not you." Sean moves in even closer to Will and continues to speak in a commanding tone, "It's not your fault." Will is becoming emotionally flooded by what he is feeling and reacting to. He covers his crying eyes and begins pushing Sean away from him. Sean responds by offering a healing touch, putting his hands on Will's shoulders. Will begins to master the flooding emotional energy and becomes aware of Sean's comforting presence as he pulls him close to him and begins sobbing, "Oh my God! I'm so sorry! I'm so sorry Sean."

Even though this is a Hollywood film, it demonstrates that dark energy is experienced by individuals who have undergone intense, emotionally-arousing situations. The personality pattern that Will displayed demonstrates how strong feelings of shame and guilt were flooding his psyche. In this chapter I will explain the pseudosexual panic symptoms and feelings that Will experienced during his unsuccessful meetings with his previous therapists.

During his initial session with a renowned psychiatrist, he began to experience underlying anxiety symptoms that generated intense emotional flooding and a defensive sexual panic reaction. Immediately he began to attribute these unwelcome sensations to his psychiatrist. This is called projection and distortion. Will's archaic base-brain protective energy field had been controlling his emotional attachments and restricting his love quests until he began a stormy healing relationship with Sean. He had been a lonely boy, trying to hide his pain by keeping company with his havoc-raising buddies and disguising his brilliance as he worked as a janitor at MIT.

BODY-RELATED ANXIETY ENERGY PATTERNS

Psychological investigations have long been examining and interpreting the relationship of the mind (psyche) and the body (soma) anxiety energy patterns that are the result of intense emotional flooding. Strong physiological reactions begin to overtake the mind and body. Difficulty expressing warm and loving feelings and sexual functioning problems often can occur. Today, if an individual displays rapid heartbeat, heavy breathing and sweats like Frankie experienced in the attack on his base, we attribute these symptoms to anxiety and panic. Our modern-day perspective that a person is a unique individual and responsible for oneself was not in the mindset of early man. He attributed these symptoms to the gods since they are out of our voluntary control. Non-rational, powerful, psychic-generating energy fields, such as anxiety and panic, were projected to the god Pan. People today continue to experience the same symptoms of anxiety, fear and panic that our predecessors felt, particularly in love and relationships. It is our views about the many ways anxiety can occur and how we can treat these symptoms that have dramatically changed.

Dr. Horsley Gantt, Pavlov's American-born protégé and behavioral health research pioneer, made a unique discovery. He proposed that we can experience anxiety symptoms because the same external stimuli that we may encounter can often generate conflicting, contradictory, conditioned responses that originate from our digestive, reproductive and cardiovascular systems. Our emotional brain can feel an attraction to someone and become sexually aroused, only to be overruled by our thinking brain. Bodily reactions to these anxiety-producing stimuli can then result in stress symptoms. We want, but for some reason we cannot have. On the other hand, our bodily reaction can become so overwhelming that it totally shuts down and becomes numb. The opposite situation can also surge as intense sexual arousal can be activated. This behavior serves as a protective, tension release mechanism and prevents our psyche from disintegrating into a psychotic state and loss of a personal self.

Gantt took Pavlov's findings one step further with his experiments on the cardiovascular system of dogs. He discovered that when they were conditioned with high-pitched sounds they became anxious and eventually reacted as traumatized. One dog, Nick, played in a normal fashion when he was living at the Gantt farm, but when brought to the laboratory he relived his anxiety to the point of experiencing involuntary panic reaction related sexual ejaculations. These symptoms lasted for years, long after the original stress had occurred. Humans have these symptoms as well, but are too uncomfortable to talk about them.

I learned about these symptoms from Danny and the many Vietnam veterans who shared with me some of these unwanted pseudo-sexual surging experiences. They would report that they felt weird and queer. Danny once told me he heard a squirrel rustling in his attic and became intensely aroused and felt as if he were back in combat. He ran for his BB gun and observed himself displaying a full erection and, at the same time, a thunderous excitement throughout his body. He killed the squirrel and immediately ejaculated. Within minutes he felt like shooting himself as well with the gun. These inner, psychic, agitated feelings are contributory to suicidal thinking and behavior.

Dr. Lionel Ovesey, a psychoanalyst, wrote articles about the power struggles that many males experience. This anxiety is felt surging beneath the chaotic energy dark patterns of the psyche as individuals strive to seal off these unwelcome emotionally flooding body sensations. Psychodynamic oriented therapists refer to this as a flight-fight response and pseudo-sexual panic. My patient Tom complained he often felt so sexually aroused that he just had to masturbate to release the sexual tension he was experiencing, even though he was really feeling intense anger and no erotic feelings whatsoever. Tom began to feel more comfortable as he learned about defensive expressive flight/fight body motor movement energy patterns that can agitate the body. It was even more helpful when he became aware of the areas of the brain located right next to each other, the septum, with its cousin, the nucleus accumbens (sexual) and the amygdala (anxiety) that fire up when we are intensely emotionally flooded.

These symptoms of unwelcome sexual stimulation and confusion can result in emotional brain generated vituperative outbursts, accusations and distortions of what is really taking place in a person's body and overtaking their mind. This state is referred to as pseudo-sexual anxiety. Remember the F-sound that I constantly heard during my navy days? The root of this expression is a verbal attempt to express and cope with these tensions and sensations flooding our mind and body. Remember Dr. Adler's playful dictum "Fighting and Fucking"? That is, sexual and aggressive arousal is generated by the same brain systems in the body. After many years of intense treatment with me, Zack, (chapter five) a wounded combat warrior, eventually acknowledged that he had killed women and children in Vietnam. He then expressed intense rage and projected sexual accusations at me as the pseudo-sexual arousal, shame and guilt he was feeling began gushing forth from him.

Harold was a political hostage who had been severely tortured and beaten by his captors. He returned home and was able to mostly recover, except that he was unable to sexually perform with his wife. The prescribed medical treatments did not work. He would call his wife an enemy imposter and all the other vituperative expletives that Zack projected to me. Rational discussion about what was taking place was useless, since this emotionally-flooded, brain-driven state has no access to the thinking self. That is why sexual panic situations are referred to as fragmental, psychotic personality patterns or ego states.

When I was evaluating Chester, who had undergone many intense combat situations in Iraq, he shared some intimate details with me and immediately drifted into a trance-like catatonic state. I had to gently coax him back to reality by activating a breathing technique that his therapist had taught him. When we met again three years later, he began drifting back and reliving these events. I ended our meeting in an attempt to prevent his re-experiencing the trauma.

Soon thereafter, he complained to his therapist that I was engaged in ridiculing, sexual, gyrating movements during our fifteen-minute interview. This probably resulted from his over-disclosure about his inadequate sexual functioning. Chester was reliving the thunderous sounds of life-threatening encounters reverberating throughout his organism, particularly in his pelvic floor area. The emotional flooding he was experiencing was just too much to take. This behavior relates to the postulation of Drs. Gantt and Ovesey concerning pseudo-sexual anxiety about situations such as this. Being able to project his unwelcome, painful emotions was nature's way of protecting Chester. He had been constantly complaining that people were making fun of him (base and limbic brain energy fields intruding in his awareness). This type of reaction results in paranoid behavior.

Chester's major comfort was to restore his self-esteem by becoming a gourmet cook and working as a park ranger.

The suspicious, hypervigilant, accusatory, defensive coping reactions that Zack, Chester, Harold and many other patients experienced are attempts to ward off and avoid the psychic and physical bombing from the horrific mayhem they encountered in battle or trauma. The Greeks were well aware of this body–mind reaction. Intense emotional energy flooding and an inability to express warm and loving feelings were the major reasons why it took the Greek warrior Odysseus so long to come home from war.

Another symptom of these anxiety states is distressing sleep patterns that manifest themselves during the rapid eye movement sleep phase called REM. The body becomes totally stiff in this stage except for a rapidly beating heart and heavy breathing. What is even more interesting about this state is, in the male, the penis throbs and becomes firm and erect. In the female, the clitoris engorges, even though the dreamer may be reliving a traumatic incident. This phenomenon is pseudo-sexual since most of the dreams in this rapid eye movement state are related to a panicky anxiety that floods the patient's sexual system. They are non-erotic and have nothing to do with pleasure. In fact, unwelcome, non-voluntary sexual arousal is a defense that the organism employs to protect itself and prevent it from "freaking out." Skip related to me an incident in which he incurred a lower back injury while parachuting during a combat mission in Afghanistan. Soon thereafter he found himself walking around with a chronic erection. No physical explanation could be medically determined and it was conjectured that his symptoms were psychological in nature. He was not allowed to re-enlist in the Army. He displayed no other symptoms. This likeable, determined young man's future plan was to become a mercenary in a war-zone. His comment was, "I just have to live with this stiff dick. It seems it has a life of its own."

Deep in the recesses of the emotional brain lie the neurons that generate the powerful energy patterns that relate to anxiety, memory and sex. These areas of the brain are located right next to each other and fire up together when a person is over-aroused. This is why people like Tom can often experience so much confusion about emotionally flooded, brain-driven conflicting neuronal sensations of pain and pleasure. Understanding how these neurons are reacting can aid in a successful recovery.

Siri Leknes reported in a neuroscience journal that the same brain circuits that activate pleasure centers are also connected to pain centers. These abreacting and surging energies are seeking release and tend to dominate our life, especially when we have been in a life-threatening situation such as war and battle. Many ex-warriors have experienced these symptoms and, if their trauma was very severe, can never get over this state of always being on the edge. It affects their ability to have warm and loving feelings and to express and engage in satisfactory committed sexual relationships. Sometimes ex-warriors experience intense sexual craving, engage in physical sexual activity, but cannot maintain a relationship, especially if they still feel that intense adrenaline rush associated with killing in battle.

My late psychoanalytic teachers and supervisors, Drs. Jock Murray and John Arsenian, postulated that there was little difference between sex and aggression when there are intensely activated, undifferentiated energy fields and bodily movements seeking release and expression. What is being expressed in sexual terms has really nothing to do with romance. Danny's story about battle and the mayhem of sexual arousal and killing is classic. Ex-warriors often feel very guilty about what they did in battle, especially the physical adrenaline and sexual arousal they experienced. Since the hippocampus (old brain memory center) is involved, confusion about what they are experiencing clouds the conscious mind. It sometimes is very difficult to sort out what is happening now from what had gone on then. New learning and concentration is seriously affected.

A survivor copes through rational and literal thinking as the mind attempts to make some sense about what has happened. A suspicious attitude is a coping mechanism to ward off the intruding trauma. The psychic pain is horrific. Vets have told me about daymares, such as what June and Danny experienced in spite of their attempts to keep busy through work and any other distracting activity. It is a life of hell. Many veterans of other wars have told me that the major positive ingredient in their recovery from horrendous trauma was the love and emotional support provided by their spouses and lovers.

"I made it through the night. My wife held me as I shivered and quaked." Another, "What the hell is wrong with me? I tried to strangle her last night."

Robert Peck, in his book *Controlling Your Hormones*, proposes that bodily reactions to traumatic events and REM sleep patterns are very much related. When our REM sleep state patterns are activated, the abrupt thunderous, booming infusion of wind, rain and fire recycles itself and breathes its vitality into us. This description is similar to the energy infusion from the Holy Spirit that the Christian apostles experienced on Pentecost. Mystics of many traditions experience this powerful energetic infusion when they activate their intense breathing, tension-release practices, such as *kriya* yoga undoing the knots and blocked bodily tensions.

The big bang explosion from which creation and the universe evolved has left its mark in our genetic makeup when we experience stress. Peck uncovered the findings of century old inner psychic science practitioners who had identified a set of muscles called the perineum that is located beneath our sex organs and extends to our anal cavity. When stressed this master body organ can manifest energy patterns that generate anxiety, panic and pseudo-sexual defensive reactions. In unison with our archaic base-brain, the perineum helps us manage our breathing, eating, moving and sexual expressive energy. Learning to control these muscles with breathing exercises such as the Circle Breath that I will share with you in chapter thirteen helps reduce the tension that can be manifested by this master body power spot.

What are your thoughts and reactions to this big bang formulation concerning the intense lower body activation of our perineum located in close proximity to our anal cavity or asshole in limbic language and vagina in females or scrotum in males? Can we really make rational sense about the scientific proposal that the world evolved from dark holes and chaos? Is that why we feel sometimes so close to, and sometimes so very anxious about, the people we love? We so much want the love of our life to be with us forever, but when this chaotic, base brain related reabsorbing energy pattern surges we become anxious. Do you believe that we can train our pelvic core muscles and acquire the skill to master our movements and sexual energy and at the same time feel the natural ecstatic joy we are all seeking? Is this why we invoke the biological functions of this control center when we release our every day tensions with the expletives of fuck, shit and piss? Dr. Candice Pert postulates that our mid-brain's Nucleus of Barrington area not only controls our pissing and shitting, but also carries a neuropeptide, CRF, that connects us to our pleasure-driven locus coeruleus neural pathway. This is why there is so much confusion and difficulty in loosening the knots of emotional trauma. Are you aware that the mystics called this sacral area the seat of wisdom? We navy medics, on the other hand, playfully proclaimed that everyone wants their ass kissed, but the only problem is it stinks. The next chapter shares my students' many exciting, and sometimes painful adventures, and my proposal on what love is all about.

12.

WHAT'S IT ALL ABOUT?
FINDING AND LIVING IN A STATE OF LOVE

CLASS TIME

In this chapter I would like to share with you my personal views on the nature of love and challenging situations I encountered while teaching courses on Personality and Counseling Theories and The Theory and Practice of Group Therapy. I have always been eager to learn if there are real scientific techniques that work and help people to deal with their issues in matters of love. Most of what I can report to you is simple. Paper and pencil evidence-based questionnaires and the research techniques of experimentally derived psychology cannot mend a broken heart. Because what love means to us is ours alone, because we each have our own unique manner of relating, because each of us expresses our love psychically and physically in our own way. Trying to analyze someone's romantic attractions and connections has its limitations.

One of the cases we study in my class is that of Gloria, an attractive, courageous, thirty-year-old divorced mother of two who agreed to be interviewed by three different master therapists in order for them to demonstrate their approaches to psychotherapy. You can now watch Carl Rogers, Albert Ellis and Fritz Perls interview Gloria on YouTube. Her issues are related to searching for and finding love on many levels. What is unique is this is a real situation. It is not staged. Today, privacy rights require that demonstrations are role-played, often with a scripted treatment approach.

Gloria asked Dr. Rogers whether she should tell her nine-year-old daughter that she lied to her about her many overnight rendezvous with gentlemen callers. He did not offer an opinion. Instead, Rogers used a person-centered approach in which he encouraged Gloria to contact her inner, feeling self, become emotionally self-trusting and make her own decisions in matters of love. Their meeting is very emotionally engaging as Gloria expresses the wish that her father would relate to her as Rogers was doing. Rogers told her she would be such a good daughter. Some of the class felt this was an inappropriate statement on Rogers's part.

Dr. Ellis was more philosophical and mildly confrontational with his rational, emotive approach that is based on the philosophy that it is not what happens to you, but your negative emotional reactions to past events that impair you in achieving your goals. He suggested that she should take more risks in finding love.

Dr. Perls attempted to engage her to express and experience her frustration and disappointments with him. She liked and hated him at the same time. Sounds familiar? His approach was too brash and upset her to tears.

My class and I shared our reactions to this love-seeking Gloria. I probed the class to express their opinions about these approaches. Their reactions were very informative and revealed a lot about their own views and experiences. The technical term is countertransference. All that means is we are emotionally and physically reacting to what we are perceiving and experiencing. If you live in "Yupville" and have a logical positivistic belief system that operates on the assumption that everything, including romantic relationships, can be rationally explained, you are ignoring the mysterious emotional brain generated energy patterns that cannot be scientifically explained.

Our class engaged in a lot of role-playing with real or imagined situations. After all, life is a drama of our experiences on many levels. Students often enjoy sharing their reactions to what they are hearing and their own stories of love. During one semester, Debbie, one of the students, shared with the class her troubled relationship with Matt. They had met in college and lived together for a few years afterwards. Matt wanted to be off on his own and they split. Deb was brokenhearted. She went home to live for a short while with mom and dad. Mom felt all her pain. Deb was her love child and had been so close to her family. She had a much younger brother, Sam, and an older half-sister, Helen, who told her to get over it. "Listen up, Deb. Mush mouth Matt is no good. He's just a self-centered mama's boy, sulky wimp who never wants to grow up."

Deb loved Helen but told her she was mean, harsh and jealous of her relationship with Matt.

"Could be true," retorted Helen. "I'm your sister and I know what that Matt is up to. In his mind you're really not good enough for him and he thinks there is something better out there for him. Listen to me. Get over him. Get a new life."

A stormy rash of breakups and reunions had been occurring for almost two years. Each time after they broke up Matt would plead to get back with Deb, only to break up again. Mom had become so upset that Deb finally promised her she would never see Matt again.

During our semester Deb told her mom that she was going on a vacation all by herself to think things over. She was, however, secretly planning to meet up again with Matt. She did. They went off on a trip together. And then, he pulled the same stunt. To make matters even more complicated Helen found out and told mom. Mom was so broken-hearted that she became very depressed. Then the awful news from dad, "Mom can't take any more of this. She never wants to speak with you again and to please leave her alone and stay away." Helen was somewhat consoling, but told Deb it had to be that way. "You have been just as selfish as Matt, putting our family and mom through this stupid craziness."

The class was very excited by this ongoing drama that

captured our attention for over two months. There were many suggestions of what to do. The students were offering advice, experimenting with the current counseling techniques being presented during each of our weekly class meetings.

Many weeks passed. Mom and dad held their ground and refused to have contact with Deb. Helen told Deb that mom was now on meds and seeing a therapist. One of her classmates asked Deb if she would see Matt again. She tearfully said yes, if he asked her.

As a "love doctor" (that is what my group therapy patients called me) I felt it was time to teach the class my moves in matters of love. There is a part of my psyche that is soft and empathic and another that has Jesuit toughness. Utilizing this paradoxical method of relating, I asked Deb if she could commit to give up going out with Matt for six months to a year to please mom, her family and the class. Some students were supportive of this approach, others thought her situation was futile and even suggested Matt had another relationship or two on the side. Deb agreed to try my strategy.

We composed two love notes: One to mom, another to Matt.

Mom's note:

Dear Mom
    I am so sorry I have not listened to you and the advice you have given me. I am such a fool and so sorry for all the trouble I have caused you. You are such a loving and caring mom and are always looking out for me. Why can I not listen to you? You are always right. Please forgive me just this one last time.
    I love you mom and I cry for you every day.

Love,

Deb

Matt's Note:

Dear Matt,

You know how much I miss you and love you
and I know and feel how much you love me too.

Am I not good enough for you or are you just
a selfish, jelly-brained bowl of mush who is afraid to
commit? This is it.

Do not attempt to see me for the next six months
and when you do I want a ring and a proposal of
marriage. This sounds harsh, but it is what you need. I
am tired of being the jerk when I know you feel deep
inside that you are one.

If something good is going to happen in our
relationship, it has to happen now. Do you get it?

Have a few beers with your buddies when you
mull over this. It can soak up the sorrow we both feel
when we break up.

Love,

Deb

PS

Say hello to your darling mom who is so happy we're
not together.

Deb followed instructions. It was painful, but she was
intent on improving her life.

After a little more than a week dad called and arranged
a family dinner. Deb felt really good and thanked the class for
all their help. She even shared her plan and letter to Matt with
Helen who promised her she would not tell mom about this
demand. Helen was so proud of her younger sister. Their bond
became stronger.

Our semester was ending. We had explored many answers,
but there will still be questions when it comes to managing
matters of the heart.

As a side note, a few years later I ran into Beth, one of the students in the class, who informed me she had recently said a quick hello to a smiling Deb and a handsome young man pushing a baby carriage at the mall. Drama from the past was moving forward to the future. Love has its own mystery, rewards and joy.

HEALING BROKEN HEARTS

Saturday mornings can be a special time for many adult learners as they unwind from their work week and become available to dialogue and explore personal or patient problems. The experiential component of our class, *The Use of the Self in Therapy*, is designed to provide an opportunity for students to share, learn and heal as they release tensions from their deepest inner psychic cores. Students often have many personal stories to share. They also conduct research on a subject they choose and present their findings to the class. The goal of the class is to refine the students' practice skills and promote improvement in their self-image. We dialogue situations and eventually create role-play scenarios to enact our life story. The healing, sharing and transformation that is experienced can be edifying and rewarding. Relationships with former lovers surge. Love stories usually create the most interest. Tears flow.

During one of our Saturday class exercises, Cora began wailing tears of pain. "He was so kind and loving. I gave up so much for him. Why does he walk by me now and totally ignore me? It is like I am a total stranger. I see him on the street almost every day. My heart is leaking tears. We were so close. I gave him every bit of me. He knew how much I loved him. Like a fool I felt he loved me in the same way. Now I'm nothing. I'm so empty, so lonely and upset. I think he does this to torture me."

After releasing this intense pain, Cora began to reflect. "The me I thought he loved was not the me, Cora. It was some kind of image of me in his head. He used me and put his energy into me. I felt him and gave him my whole self. It is awful, ugly and painful. That feeling still runs through me. It hurts so much."

As she related her painful experience some of the women offered her their gentle healing touch. I felt her feelings of being abandoned and rejected. There were no words to say, just a caring presence to provide.

Cora thanked the class for listening to her story and continued discussing being abandoned by Albert. Each had been in painful relationships before. He had a history of dumping and love-seeking in the past. Cora had also been disappointed in previous romantic involvements. Albert was the best lover she had ever had and had made her feel so good. He just upped and left her. No talk, just left. Pain set in. Her sorrow and loss were unbearable.

In a quiet, restorative and reflective state, Cora concluded the hour session with her self-appraisal. "I'm getting smart. I am so good, beautiful and energized. I have to be more aware about being duped and getting involved with someone who doesn't treat me right. It still hurts, but I feel much better thanks to you wonderful, caring friends." The group supported her in what had happened to her and her new perception of her experience. A renewed psychic energy began to flow.

Within the next few minutes Uma burst out crying, "You, at least, were able to feel and share love. I was never allowed to feel the love that you had with Al, your man. Where I came from young girls are sexually mutilated. It is horrible. I had to get away from that world. I don't want this to happen to anyone. I had my kids here. Remembering my days back home and the way women are treated makes me sick."

We all sat in silence. It was interesting that no students felt Uma wanted to be touched or hugged. We continued in the silence and after a short while I asked her if there was something she wanted to do about it. She replied that she wanted to change this practice. She eventually wrote a very comprehensive research paper on female circumcision practices in Africa. The class was very impressed with her authentic sharing.

My view of my role in these students' expressions of their experiences is that of a facilitator for nature's restorative energy that elevates us from the dark, chaotic side of our psyche to our natural state of growth, love and connection. These dark, primary, emotional flooding sensations cannot often be described verbally, but recede into a world without words. Experiencing this dark energy is so confusing since the pain of the event can often set off defensive, unwanted and weird feeling sexual sensations. In order to cope with this intense intrusion, a person's psyche freezes over and survives by becoming numb and behaving as if nothing ever happened. In time, surging rage can begin to erupt as the frozen buried dark energy resurfaces. This pattern continues in a vicious circle until the tension is released.

Such is the way of the dark side of love's chaotic manifestation. In the company of caring, loving people the tension will release and the dark knots begin to loosen and thaw. At other times it is better to keep these destructive and maddening energy fields from being expressed, since they will create more chaos. Medication can often dampen these ugly sensations. The evil shadow of that negative energetic flow sits deep in the archaic recesses of our psyche, torturing and tormenting us with exciting, lustful, energetic expressions. They offer a momentary pleasure, but eventually bring about our demise. Our thinking self, as Cora explained, must contain, control and evaluate the risks associated with the painful dark side of love as we play with and engage in these irresistible attractions. We can even push this intruding energy far away from our awareness and delude ourselves by denying the existence of this shadow of our mind. Expressions of love can be so thrilling and exciting sometimes, and painful and disappointing at other times.

John Twomey

SO WHAT IS LOVE?

Tell me, if love so nice, tell me why it hurt so bad.
If I love, love so nice, tell me, tell me why I'm sad?

Junior Kelly (Reggæ Song)

Do you remember Guppy, the great lover of a thousand years ago? My experience of observing and interacting with thousands of people for many decades has drawn me to his approach. I would like to share it with you. Guppy simply stated that love is our awareness of Mother Nature's ecstatic, pulsating energy flowing through us. So we just have to train ourselves to access and listen to this natural, nonverbal energy streaming through us. It moves like the wind with positive and negative vectors of energy patterns, sometimes still and other times blowing with devastating and destructive intensities. We can feel on top of the world as we are experiencing this natural flow pouring through us. In our many ways of expressing love we nourish ourselves as we inhale and exhale these heart-throbbing sensations pulsating in the very core of our being. It is constantly vibrating joyous, heavenly bubbles, floating and rippling waves of light and sound. We emerge from this experience with a restored and renewed sense of self. This life-generating pattern is like a flowing stream, sometimes very active and other times still.

Expressive love energy patterns have their own complexities. Remember all of our love stories related to inner subjective mood states called qualia that can last for hours and even days? What they scientifically mean remains a mystery. Researchers have been unable to satisfactorily explain these exciting and sad feelings that we experience in our love connections. Love is really nice, but a piercing hurt also floats into the picture. Is it because of our attachment to our lover? Do we feel we are going to be ridiculed or rejected in some fashion? Or what is even worse, dumped. It is like death, an emptiness, nothing.

It seems that emotionally generated base-brain primary expressions like fuck and shit are attempting to express and mimic our natural, innate, dark, chaotic energy field patterns. That is why I refer to the F-sound as the grand mantra. It is a human being directing, invoking or cursing with this naturally pulsating energy that is always subtly sitting beneath the background of our base brain, vibrating the creative (*fac* or fuck) and the chaotic dissolution (shit) component of our nature. We can be very offended by these sounds since they are so primal and truthful. Our personal psychic space is invaded and we have to shut down or dissociate and block this energy field in order to function in a realistic frame of mind and existence.

Living life is like dancing with this constant creative energy flowing through us. Sometimes it excites us with its ecstatic arousal. Its other side is that lethargic, shadowy, shitty side, our energy contracting that surfaces when we are rejected or lose a significant person in our lives, especially in matters of love. Loss and separation make us aware that we are only physically interacting with those we love for a short while, but emotionally, we are connected forever. That is why we explode on the people we love the most. Plato called this a divine disease since there are conflicting and opposing forces of creation that are seeking reconciliation. For example, Frankie and Molly's romantic connection and all the spazzing that would occur.

This way of observing the world and our relationship to it is called transpersonal psychology. It simply means that there is more to us than our physical body and that we are all connected to each other and to the mysterious life force in a psychic way. Each of us, as individuals, has a drop of this vital force that generates our quest for finding love with all of its drama and anticipatory excitement. It surges so intensely when we are feeling most passionately connected with people we love. It deflates painfully when our connection is broken. Junior Kelly laments what science cannot explain: "Tell me if love so nice. Tell me why it hurt so bad. If love, love, so nice. Tell me, tell me why I'm sad."

13.

THE CIRCLE BREATH EXERCISE: ACCESSING AND ELEVATING YOUR NATURALLY FLOWING ENERGY

Remember the introduction to this book that asks if you ever find yourself longing for a happy state of enchantment, love and connection? Do you now observe your rationally thinking mind constantly attempting to find a reason for your emotional brain-driven hungry heart's love searching desires? Throughout this book I have described my approach to understanding our individual manner of relating and seeking psychic fulfillment through observing our unique nonverbal old brain driven primary communication patterns that we unconsciously display during our daily activities and relationships. As we are living our life we are inhaling and exhaling our naturally driven vibrating energy fields inviting and directing us to glow, (feel the beauty) and grow (expand and master) our evolving neurotransmitter and hormonally driven expressions for love and connection.

Can we access all this energy flowing within us? Yes. I will share some exercises that can activate your dormant energy patterns so you can relate to your surroundings and experience love in the ways that attract you. You will acquire skill in mastering the ups and downs of love. Your emotional brain transmits its natural smile, stilling the busy inner chatter of your mind. You release your psychic pains of the past and ignite the flame of love dwelling within you.

You will do some inner self-reflection as you gently tune into the sensations flowing through your body. Are other people's energy fields intruding on your mind, invading your personal space and placing demands on you? Do you want to let them go? Are you dreaming of finding love, beauty and completeness? Make a few notes or keep a journal if you like.

Are your moods affecting how you think and what you want? Do you have grudges from the past limiting your expression and relating patterns? What do you want to change in your life? One of the outcomes of these exercises is to activate your restorative energy patterns and release the knots jamming your brain's neural networks.

This exercise connects you to the psychic centers that activate the power spots in your brain, forehead, throat, heart, abdomen, genitals and pelvic core. It is called the Circle Breath. You observe the energy patterns continuously flowing with your breath into the power spots down the front of your body and up your back to the top of your head. Your individual self melts into a relaxing trance as you contact transformative, inner psychic energy fields that lie quietly beneath your everyday awareness and are the seat of the love deep within you.

Circle Breath Exercise

Make yourself comfortable. Sit up straight in your chair. You can also lie on your back, but you may become too sleepy. Ignore the chatter of your busy self-talk trying to interfere with your moving into a quiet space. Be aware that this exercise is just about the love that is within you waiting to emerge. Make yourself feel whole. If your mind starts to race, try not to follow its attempts to grab your attention and channel you into a thinking mode. Tell your mind to be still. Your goal is to relax and let your inner psychic creative energy field expand, elevate and grow.

1. As you sit in your chair, slowly take in a breath and hold it for a few seconds, then breathe out. Now breathe in deeply through your nose, allowing your breath to rise up through your forehead to the top of your head. Slowly exhale. Take another breath into your chest. Hold it for a few seconds then slowly exhale. Place your hands on your chest and feel the space where you just exhaled. Do this a

few times. Do not hurry. Try not to think. Relax.

2. Take in a deep breath and try to let that air fill your abdomen. Hold your breath for a few seconds and relax. You may place your hands on your abdomen to feel the flow. Do this a few times. Relax.

3. Now try moving your breath from your abdomen down to the base of your spine. This is your sacral core area. Be aware of a very gentle fluctuation at the base of your spine, moving back on your in breath and forward on your out breath.

4. As you gradually become aware of this core center at the base of your spine, gently coax your breath to rise up your spine to the top of your head. As you slowly breathe out you will discover that you are becoming more relaxed each time you exhale. Repeat this breathing pattern a few times, drawing your breath into your chest, through your abdomen to the base of your spine, and then allow it to rise up your spine in a gentle exhale.

5. Take in a deep breath and feel your heart beating. Let life's love-flowing energy breathe through you. You can repeat to yourself, "My heart beats slow and regular. My heart beats slow and regular." Be aware that love's life force energy is breathing you, releasing your tensions and elevating your energy patterns. Try to observe that there is a short pause after your breath floats out and before it begins to come back in. When you breathe in, there is also a millisecond pause before your breath begins its journey out. This natural rhythmic pattern is similar to the cycle of the ocean tide flowing in and out. Continue to pay attention to the pause in your breath as you inhale and exhale. A magical power descends upon you as you become aware that this life force energy is breathing you. Feel the sweetness of love in your heart.

6. Every time you exhale, you are releasing your negative thoughts and loosening the knots from your mind and body. Feel the sweet love and tranquility pulsating in your heart. If you still find yourself agitated and your mind is racing with interfering thoughts, try this calming technique. Cover one nostril and inhale a few times into the other nostril, then exhale. Do the same exercise on the other

side. This will help you to become more relaxed. Do this a few times. Then slowly breathe in through both nostrils up to your forehead. As you exhale your agitation will begin to recede.

A SELF-REGULATING RELAXING EXERCISE

Another technique to complement the circle breath exercise and help reduce anxiety and agitation is a century old energy regulating exercise called autogenic training. This is a series of self talk, calming body suggestions that activate your innate capacity to restore yourself to a state of love and tranquility. Begin this exercise by silently saying to yourself the first self-suggestion until you feel comfortable practicing it. Then slowly add one self-suggestion at a time. Soon you will discover you are mastering your body's energetic expressions. This will lead to a feeling of comfort and peace.

1. I am at peace. I am at peace.
   My arms and legs are heavy and warm. My arms and legs are heavy and warm.

2. My entire body is heavy and warm. My entire body is heavy and warm.

3. My entire body breathes me. It breathes me. My entire body breathes me.
   I am at peace. I am at peace.

4. My abdomen is warm. My abdomen is warm.
   I am at peace. I am at peace.

5. My heart beats slow and regular. My heart beats slow and regular.
   I am at peace. I am at peace.

6. My entire body breathes me. It breathes me.
   My entire body breathes me. It breathes me.

7. My forehead is cool. My forehead is cool.
   I am at peace. Love's energy is flowing through me.
   I am at peace. Love's energy is flowing through me.

MOVING FORWARD

If you find yourself analyzing and trying to make logical sense of your experience, become aware of your breathing. Direct your attention to the stillness sitting inside you watching everything you do. Your composed inner self has much to reveal and unravel. As this progresses you will find a deeper inner awareness of who you really are and what you really want. During these exercises your restorative energy fields are elevating and channeling you into your natural state of love and tranquility. The closeness and connection you are seeking will slowly become more available for you as your emotional brain, heartbeat and mind begin to synchronize. These breathing exercises activate your energy fields and enrich your life's experiences in whatever you choose to do. Do these exercises for as long as you want and slowly expand the time as you feel more comfortable.

The peace and love you feel when you merge your mind with nature's energetic flow can alter your perspective and offer you many new opportunities. Your newly enriched creative and intuitive discoveries may spark your interest in new explorations and adventures. You may even wish to expand and share the very personal inner psychic expressive energy patterns of your love with someone for whom you may feel an attraction or connection. Love can happen anywhere. Where and how it happens is mysterious. I wish you well in your journey to connect to your natural happy state of love's forever renewing creative manifestation in all aspects of your life, even in your quest to find that romantic love connection that your heart may be yearning for.

NOTES AND REFERENCES

CHAPTER 1

Description of Greek Personality Terms

1. *ATE* is a trance pattern that refers to what level of awareness is present when someone is performing an activity. Are they acting in a rational reflective manner or in an emotional automatic manner? Have they been taken over or induced by a trance from the gods or another human being? The Greeks referred to *ate* as a state of mind that excites us, arouses us and creates bewilderment and confusion. It was sent to man by the gods. We would refer to this today as a hypnotic state. In this *ate* state behavior is not intentional or rational. It is intense and emotional. In our present psychological terminology we would attribute it to behavior that is being dominated by neurotransmitters or hormones being activated by our emotional brain that has an energy system not primarily connected to our thinking self. In matters of love, there are so many examples in which people are dominated by *ate*. This is the driving energy that can make one happy one moment and miserable in another. Guilt is an important feeling that often surges after one experiences *ate*. Frankie's situation with Patricia certainly demonstrated this madness and all its complexities.

2. *MENOS* was the term the Greeks used to describe the direct empowerment by, and communication from, the gods to humans. In this state an individual feels menos primarily in his or her chest. *Menos* is the mysterious infusion of a creative, powerful energy that inspires confidence and eagerness. This playful, inventive energy is quite mysterious. It was ascribed to the gods since it is so unpredictable and originates from some unidentifiable source. Our present day psychological terminology would describe *menos* as being derived from the emotional brain, as is *ate*. A person simply acts and responds in a manner that is not cognitive and rational, but is rather in a transcendent, life force expressive state. Frankie certainly experienced this state many times in Vietnam as he solved

problems in intuitive and untraditional ways. His decision to not shoot the two men on the bridge was generated from this mysterious expressive pattern.

3. *THYMOS* is the major mind–body component or state of the *psyche* and *soma*. It was believed to reside in the chest and heart area because this is where sensations are mostly felt. The *thymos* was thought to be the internal organ of feeling, an energy center of joy, excitement, pain and sorrow. It is from one's *thymos* that one takes action. This *thymos* is a command center in one's body. It is what one talks with, argues with. There can be more than one inner voice. Frankie listened to his *thymos* more than the rational, cognitive methods of his navy superiors. His love, care and duty were generated from this psychic center. In modern psychology we refer to these different inner voices as ego states. One part of the self is thinking rationally, the other emotionally. The emotional self wants to express itself. It is being restrained or "sat on" by a more reflective, thinking self. An inner psychic battle ensues. Modern psychotherapeutic techniques such as psychodrama and Gestalt therapy attempt to provide a forum to resolve and process these conflicts. As in ancient times, one still pays great attention to one's *thymos*. In fact, a person is referred to as being euthymic if one is in a happy mood, or dysthymic if in a sad or depressed mood.

4. *ETOR* is a term referring to the area in one's guts, stomach or belly, the gastrointestinal tract. Most individuals have experienced intense stomach cramps when something is not going right in their lives. Uncomfortable "pit of the stomach" sensations often accompany unpleasant events. Nervous anticipation before an anxiety-provoking event is often referred to as butterflies in the stomach. Urges to vomit, urinate or defecate are the body's attempts to rid itself of this sensation and neutralize its energy. Frankie frequently would not eat for days due to the intense stress he was experiencing.

5. *PHRENES* refers to changes in breathing and respiration. Sappho, the ancient Greek poet, wrote of feelings of love, torture and anxiety, saying that the storm of love stirs her phrenes as a

hurricane blows a fierce wind at an oak tree. We can recall Frankie's description of the many alterations in his breathing patterns. The joy that the sailor Ryan displayed in showing off his tattoos one moment and crying about his injury and the anticipated reaction of his wife shortly thereafter, demonstrates how feelings, breathing, emotions and thinking, can be interrelated

6. *KARDIA* refers to the heart. It is here that the source of anxiety, suspiciousness and seclusiveness resonate in our physical body. When we are being real and authentic we are considered to be speaking from the heart. In matters of love we want our heart to be beating close to our beloved. When we speak from the heart we are considered to be loving, open and honest. When someone is experiencing tachycardia they have a rapid heartbeat. This is related to anxiety and panic. Frankie experienced this psychic center in his many military encounters. Later in life he underwent many coronary procedures to deal with the effects of the stress generated by these events.

CHAPTER 3

The neurotransmitters: our biochemical messengers coloquially referred to as our juices.

GREENJUICE: Dopamine	Relates to emotions, perceptions and intense love. Too much: over-active brain, hallucinations and delusions. Too little: the shakes, as in Parkinson's disease.
YELLOW JUICE: Serotonin	Relates to mood, sleep, eating and blood pressure. Too little: depression and sleepiness.
BLUE JUICE: Noradrenaline Norepinephrine	Relates to wakefulness, mood, emotional states, and energy. Too much: generates anxiety and jumpiness. Too little: sleepy, depressed feeling.
PURPLE JUICE: Acetylcholine	Relates to arousal, capacity for learning and memory. Too little: confusion, poor memory and learning problems.
PINK JUICE: GABA	Relates to slowing down brain activity. Too much: sleepiness, Too little: anxious and over-excited.
BROWN JUICE: Glutamate	Relates to exciting the brain. Too much: anxiety, over excitability. Too little: sleepiness and lethargy.

1. Becker, Ernest, *Denial of Death*. (New York: Simon and Schuster, 2007).

2. Pert, Candice, *The Molecules of Emotion*. (New York: Scribner, 1997).

3. Pinker, Steven, "What the F****?" *New Republic Magazine*, (October 8, 2007).

4. Pinker, Steven, "What the F****?" *The Harvard Brain*, (2008): 20–24, 32.

CHAPTER 4

1. Adler, Stephanie and Max Day, "Learning to do Psychotherapy with Psychotic Patients: In Memory of Elvin Semrad," *Psychiatric Times*, (February 5, 2010).

2. Arsenian, John and Elvin Semrad, "Schizophrenia and Language," *Psychiatric Quarterly*, vol. 40. (1966): 449–464.

3. Gilmore, John V. *The Productive Personality*. (London: Albion Publishing, 1974).

4. Jackson, J.H. "On the Anatomical and Physiological Localization of Movements in the Brain." In *Selected Writings of John Hughlings Jackson*, edited by J. Taylor (New York: Basic Books, 1958).

5. Murray, John M. "Narcissism and the Ego Ideal," *Journal of the American Psychoanalytic Association*, vol. 12 (1964): 477–511.

6. Shultz, Johann and Wolfgang Luthe, *Autogenic Training, Psychophysiological Approach in Psychotherapy*. (New York: Grune and Stratton, 1959).

7. Sifneos, Peter. *Short Term Dynamic Psychotherapy: Evaluation and Technique*. (New York: Springer, 1979).

CHAPTER 5

1.Hubbard, L. Ron. Dianetics: *The Modern Science of Mental Health*.

(Los Angeles: Bridge Publications, 1950, 2000).

2. Schnurr, Paula, M.J. Friedman, D.W. Foy, M.T. Shea, F.Y. Hsieh, and P.W. Lavori. "Randomized Trial of Trauma-focused Group Therapy for Posttraumatic Stress Disorder," *Arch General Psychiatry*, 60 (2003): 481–489.

CHAPTER 6

1. Avalon, Arthur. *The Serpent Power*. (New York: Dover Publications, 1974).

2. Caldwell, Sara. "The Heart of the Secret: A Personal and Scholarly Encounter with Shakta Tantrism," *Nova Religio*, vol. 5, nbr. 1 (2001): 9–51.

3. Campbell, Joseph. *The Mythic Image*. (The Bollinger Foundation: Princeton University Press, 1982).

4. Kramer, Peter. *Against Depression*. (New York: Penguin Group, 2005).

CHAPTER 7

THE DESCENT OF THE VIP GODTS

Many times during my career I felt like saying something to some of the powerful administrators about their behavior. They tended to act in a powerful, punitive and grandiose way and could often generate unnecessary anxiety. As a result, these godts in their horse's ass manner of relating can often impair the very task that they are attempting to manage. In the waiting room one day a managerial team was counseling, but really admonishing, a clerk who had spoken to a local politician about patient care issues. This knowledgeable, grandiose-acting team had no awareness that their behavior was generating tension and anxiety resulting in an adverse effect on everyone around, particularly the patients. I came on the scene and could feel their arrogance and tension-generating tone permeating the area. "What should I do? How can I get these people to stop and leave? I need to get things back to normal." I knew if I spoke to them they would be offended and consider me out of order, deterring their extremely important administrative task. After all they knew more than I.

As luck would have it, a new situation developed right at the scene. Mr. X, an elderly lobotomized patient arrived, requesting help because he had soiled his pants. "Just stand right here," I said to him as the nauseating stench was becoming overwhelming. The VIP administrators remained in their self-absorbed bubble, unaware of this new situation, continuing their admonishment to the clerk for a good five minutes. Suddenly, their olfactory senses overtook their arrogance. They gaped at each other, their mouths stilled. They had been "blessed" with an olfactory transmission that totally altered their very important mission. This surging, putrid scent had cut right through their criticizing arrogance and totally altered their behavior. They now looked bewildered and befuddled. Their only sound was an OOOH as they made haste to exit the area. They said no words or made any apology for their sudden retreat.

The patients who were sitting nearby were totally entertained by the humbled and confused expression of the godts being injected with the sweet showering of putrid perfume. What was once so tense turned into joyful mirth. The soiled patient was treated by the nursing staff and happily went on his way. He had no awareness that his problem turned into the resolution of a complex situation. Needless to say, there was no further discussion. The clerk resumed his duties. The VIP godts never set foot in his workspace again.

1. Becker, Ernest. *Denial of Death*. (New York: Simon and Schuster, 1973).

2. Berne, Eric. *Transactional Analysis in Psychotherapy*. (New York: Grove Press, 1961).

3. Darwin, Charles. *Expressions of the Emotions in Man and Animals*; Commentary by Paul Ekman (3rd ed.). (New York: Oxford University Press, 1998) (Original publication 1872).

4. Dodd, Eric. *The Greeks and the Irrational*. (London: University of California Press, 1951).

5. Federn, Paul. *Ego Psychology and the Psychoses.* (New York: Basic Books, 1952).

CHAPTER 8

1. Dodd, Eric. *The Greeks and the Irrational.* (London: University of California Press, 1951).

2. Jaynes, Julian. *The Origin of Consciousness in the Breakdown of the Bicameral Mind.* (Boston: Houghton-Mifflin Company, 1990).

3. MacLean, Paul. *The Triune Brain in Evolution.* (New York: Plenum Press, 1990).

4. Rosenbaum, David. "The Cinderella of Psychology: The Neglect of Motor Control in the Science of Mental Life and Behavior," *American Psychologist*, vol. 60.4, (May 2005): 308–317.

5. Tepe, Victoria, Alison Cernich, James Kelly. "Polytraumatic Traumatic Brain Injury," *Psychiatric Annals*, 43.7, (July 2013): 309–312.

6. Tupper, David and Sandra Sondell. *Motor Disorders and Neuropsychological Development: A Historical Appreciation in Developmental Motor Disorders*, edited by Dewey, Deborah and David Tupper. (New York: The Guilford Press, 2004).

7. Watzlawick, Paul, Janet Beavin, and Don Jackson. *Pragmatics of Human Communication.* (New York: W.W. Norton & Company, 1967).

CHAPTER 9

1. Nicholas Steno (a.k.a. Niles Stenson) (1638–1686 AD) further investigated the hypotheses of Descartes. He conducted empirical tests on the pineal gland as the "master" gland and found no evidence to support Descartes' theory of its centrality to the mind's function. This was the beginning of empirically validating hypotheses about human anatomy.

2. Thomas Willis (1621–1675 AD) a chemist, anatomist and physiologist, classified the cranial nerves and coined the term vagus for the wandering nerve described by Galen 1500 years previously.

3. Jacques Winslow (1669–1760 AD) investigated "sympathetic" nerves, a concept originated in ancient Greece. He called the ganglia between the many nerves "little brains." As new ideas developed, metaphors began to change. Scientists were no longer satisfied with the term "animal spirits" which could not be empirically demonstrated. As a result of this dissatisfaction with such vague terms they created names such as nerves. These nerves were seen as being like metal wires or the strings of musical instruments that vibrated and transmitted energy to the brain.

4. Marie François Bichat (1771–1802 AD) postulated that the little brains described by Winslow functioned independently of the brain and spinal cord. His conclusion was that these little brains controlled our visceral states and passions.

5. Johann Purkinje (1787–1869 AD) and Theodor Schwann (1810–1882 AD) pioneered the use of physiological laboratories and proposed that all living organisms were made up of cells.

6. Franz Gall (1759-1828 AD) contended that the brain was the instrument or organ of the mind. Gall's initial research examined the skulls of malfunctioning individuals. He claimed that he was able to formulate a personality diagnosis by examining an individual's physical characteristics through measuring the bumps in a person's skull. Gall theorized that all intellectual functions took place in the brain's frontal lobes and determined a person's intelligence. His work turned, however, from scientific investigations of the brain to a public display of showmanship. People paid large sums of money to have their skulls analyzed. Successful lifestyles and brain typologies were formulated from an analysis of the client's skull. As this group hysteria escalated into a cult-like phenomenon, societies of craniology and phrenology were founded throughout Europe and the U.S.

7. M.J.P. Flourens (1794–1867 AD) opposed Gall's formulations

and stated that the entire brain was the major organ associated with thought and reflection in humans. He allowed that there may be special functioning in various parts of the brain, but insisted that it works together in a holistic fashion.

8. Paul Broca (1824–1880 AD), was influenced by Gall, and demonstrated that frontal brain lobe damage was related to loss of speech. He presented the case of a patient who could say only "tan" and no other words. He could, however, understand what was said to him. The patient died six days after Boca's presentation. An autopsy was conducted and revealed that the left hemisphere's frontal lobes were damaged. This confirmed Gall's theory that language is located in the frontal lobes of the brain. In Germany, Carl Wernicke demonstrated another kind of aphasia. In this type a person could be very verbal, but not understand what he/she was saying. There were speculations that the left frontal lobes of the brain grew faster than the right. Broca postulated that one speaks with the left half of the brain in the same manner that one writes with only one dominant hand. The conjecture at that time was that the right side of the brain was related to emotional and other uncontrollable urges. Individuals who were non-adaptive were viewed as right brain dominant. Eventually, it was proposed that perception and attention deficits could be related to spatial and right brain problems. Popular psychology then began to categorize the left versus right brain functioning with such descriptions as verbal and logical for left-brain prone individuals and emotional, holistic, artistic for right brain dominant people. Much of what was then formulated is still valid today.

9. J. Hughlings Jackson (1835–1911 AD) a practicing British neurologist who had conducted major research on epilepsy, but also had strong philosophical interests, entered the fray. He warned that the whole idea of trying to locate something mental in the physical was poor science. His view of the mind was revolutionary. Heavily influenced by the philosopher psychologist Herbert Spencer, Jackson proposed that the human brain had evolved over a period of time into a complex system. Lower brain centers gradually developed into more complex structures. Rational thinking, awareness and

reflection are at a higher state than the automatic or instinctive functions of the original brain. Jackson's tenet was that a healthy brain was needed to control and keep down the brute-brain in us all. Containment and mastery of impulses were the tasks of the evolved higher centers of the brain. Mental illness was viewed as a "welling up" of lower, archaic brain states. Jackson's postulations are still valid today.

10. William James of Harvard University (1842–1910 AD) also investigated and developed theories of the mind and brain, particularly in reference to the primary seat of emotion in the brain. He contended that emotion was experienced as a result of physical changes in our body and was not experienced in a special area of our brain. He said, "We feel sorry because we cry, angry because we strike, afraid because we tremble; not that we cry, strike or tremble because we are sorry angry or fearful." The physiological state precedes the psychological. We might see a bear and think it was best to run, but we would not actually feel afraid. The feeling of fear as an emotion would be experienced in the rapid heartbeat, shortness of breath and butterflies in the stomach. Without these bodily and visceral changes the perception of an emotional stimulus would be cognitive and unemotional. James was quick to point out that there is a strong connection between memory, imagination and emotion. "One can get angrier in thinking over one's insult than at the moment of receiving it."

11. Walter Cannon (1871–1910 AD) presented an opposing point of view, asserting that we often experience the fear first and the accompanying shaking later. For example, we experience the same physical reaction to very different emotions. We seem to tremble in the same manner whether frightened, excited or smitten by love. There could, therefore, be a possible location in the brain for emotions. Bodily feedback would then be a central factor in conducting an assessment of emotional states. From his experimentation he concluded that the hypothalamic area in the brain was the center of emotional arousal.

12. James Papez (1883–1958 AD) proposed that the center of

emotional experience was located in brain regions that were related to the smell and taste area, for feeding and mating were major components of ancestral brain structures.

1. Barber, Theodore. *Hypnosis: A Scientific Approach.* (New York: Van Nostrand, 1969).

2. Baudouin, Charles. *Suggestion and Autosuggestion.* (London: George Allen & Unwin Ltd., 1962).

3. Beaumont, J. Graham. *Introduction to Neuropsychology.* (New York: The Guilford Press, 1983).

4. Corsi, Pietro, ed. *The Enchanted Loom: Chapters in the History of Neuroscience.* (New York: Oxford University Press, 1991).

5. Corsini, Raymond and Danny Wedding, eds. *Current Psychotherapies*, 10th ed. (California: Brooks/Cole, CENGAGE Learning, 2014).

6. Eccles, John, ed. *The Mind and Brain.* (Washington: Paragon House, 1975).

7. Hilgard, Ernest (Jack). *Divided Consciousness: Multiple Controls in Human Thought and Action.* (New York: Wiley series in behavior, 1986).

8. Jaynes, Julian. *The Origin of Consciousness in the Breakdown of the Bicameral Mind.* (Boston: Houghton-Mifflin Company, 1990).

9. Kerr, John. *A Most Dangerous Method: The Story of Jung, Freud and Sabina Spielrein.* (New York: Vintage, 1994).

10. Leknes, Siri and Irene Tracey. "A Common Neurobiology for Pain and Pleasure," *Nature Reviews Neuroscience*, vol. 9.4, (2008): 314–320.

11. MacLean, Paul. *The Triune Brain in Evolution.* (New York: Plenum Press, 1990).

12. Rosenzweig, Saul. "Some Implicit Common Factors in Diverse

Methods of Psychotherapy," *American Journal of Orthopsychiatry*, vol. 6, (1936): 412–415.

13. Wack, Mary. *Lovesickness in the Middle Ages*. (Philadelphia: University of Pennsylvania, 1990).

CHAPTER 11

1. McGuigan, Frank and Thomas Ban, eds. *Critical Issues in Psychiatry and Physiology: A Memorial to W. Horsley Gantt*. (New York: Gordon and Breach Science, 1987).

2. Leknes, Siri and Irene Tracy. "A Common Neurobiology for Pain and Pleasure," *Nature Reviews Neuroscience*, vol. 9.4 (2008): 314–320.

3. Ovesey, Lionel. "Pseudosexuality, The Paranoid Mechanism and Paranoia," *Psychiatry*, vol. 18, (1955): 163–175.

4. Peck, Robert. *Controlling Your Hormones*. (Lebanon, Connecticut: Personal Development Center, 2008).

5. Pert, Candice. *The Molecules of Emotion*. (New York: Scribner, 1997).

CHAPTER 12

1. Dodd, Eric. *The Greeks and the Irrational*. (London: University of California Press, 1953).

2. Jaynes, Julian. *The Origin of Consciousness in the Breakdown of the Bicameral Mind*. (Boston: Houghton-Mifflin Company, 1990).

3. Shultz, Johann and Wolfgang Luthe. *Autogenic Training: A Psychophysiological Approach in Psychotherapy*. (New York: Grune and Stratton, 1959).

4. Taylor, Eugene. *The Mystery of Personality*. (New York: Springer, 2009).

GLOSSARY

ATE: A classic Greek metaphor that describes surging, erotic excitement, arousal and bewilderment. Neurotransmitters and opiates are the biological correlates in this process.

AMYGDALA: An almond-shaped area beneath the ears in the left and right sides of the brain that signals anxiety when we are experiencing stress.

BASAL GANGLIA: Knot-like masses of gray matter that sit deep beneath our forebrain. They activate our neurotransmitters and also our needs for organization and routines.

BLUE JUICE: Noradrenaline relates to the arousal and memory molecules in the brain. You need this juice to become alert and wakeful.

BROWN JUICE: Glutamate aids in memory formation.

CEREBELLUM: Area of our midbrain relating to posture, muscle movement and balance.

DIANETICS: A therapeutic approach advocated by L. Ron Hubbard in the 1950s that uncovers traumatic events and memories from the past. A person's tensions are activated and released through a technique called auditing. The expected result is that a person will then see things clearly and live their life in a high state of awareness and satisfaction.

EGO STATE: A state of consciousness that alters depending on which neurotransmitters are dominant at the time. It can be our thinking, rational brain or our emotionally-driven, love searching brain.

ENERGY FIELD: The unique methods by which your body, mind and brain vibrate, energize, learn, and connect to the world around you.

ENDORPHINS: Neuropeptides, "Me Juice," since it makes one feel good after an exciting, rewarding activity.

EUPHORIA: Feeling happy and energized

Frontal brain: One of the four lobes in the forebrain that serves as a major area in our decision-making, feeling, imagination and control.

GREEN JUICE: Dopamine's activity generates excitement. The main pathways of this juice arise in the mysterious striped center in the brain.

HIPPOCAMPUS: The "sea horse" area in our temporal lobes related to memory.

HOLY PICTURES: Metaphor for pornographic pictures.

HOLY WATER: Metaphor for beer.

HYPOTHALAMUS: A mini-control cluster of neurons or center through which our primary emotional energy such as mating, fighting and fleeing takes place.

KUNDALITIS: My playful metaphor to describe incessant love-seeking behavior as a disease. It is our base brain's manifestation of a constant recycling, mysterious, pulsating, sexually expressive energy pattern that needs to be mastered in order to function. This energy functions in a manner similar to the scientific principles of the recirculating nitrogen and oxygen cycles that simply state energy recirculates and cannot be created or destroyed.

LATERALIZED BRAIN: The left side of the brain usually controls the right side of the body, while the right brain controls the left side and sometimes the right side of the body. We tend to lateralize when we analyze or intellectualize. I refer to this colloquially as Yup.

LIMBIC LANGUAGE: Words and expletives that never change. They are intensely expressed during overwhelming highly pleasurable and painfully disappointing situations.

LIMBIC SYSTEM: An older set of brain structures that lie beneath the newer cerebral frontal brain. It is also called the nose brain, smell brain or visceral brain. There are areas nearby that connect to clusters of nerves that relate to memory, feelings and sexuality.

MEDULLA: It connects our brain to our spinal cord. This network relates to our automatic involuntary breathing, heartbeat, waking, sleeping, swallowing and sexual patterns.

MENOS: An early coined Greek term describing the infusion of a creative, powerful mysterious energy that inspires confidence and eagerness.

NEUROKINETIC SIGNATURE EXPRESSION OR ENERGY FIELD PATTERNS: The unique methods by which your body, mind, and brain vibrate, energize and connect to the world around you.

NEURON: Nerve cells that receive, analyze and transmit information. Firing, connecting, exciting and competing is the neuron's play in our lifestyle.

NEUROTRANSMITTERS: "Juices" travel across the synaptic cleft, a small gap between the neurons and have a major influence on mood, attention and memory.

OCCIPITAL LOBES: The part of the brain in the back of the head where vision is processed.

PARIETAL LOBES: The part of the brain where bodily sensations are experienced.

PINK JUICE: GABA, an amino acid that slows down the brain's electrical activity. Too much brain activity brings on a spaz.

PERINEUM: The area of the body between the vagina and the anus in females and scrotum and anus in males.

PONS: The area in our brain stem that relates to our waking and sleeping.

PREFRONTAL CORTEX: Frontal areas of the brain where we concentrate, plan, reflect, and modify our behavior.

PSYCHONEUROLOGY: Metaphors of the brain to describe psychological and biological behavior much in the same way the ancient Greeks coined their terms.

Purple juice: Acetylcholine relates to acquiring and maintaining memory, too much brings on agitation, too little, stupor.

QUALIA: Subjective mood states that can last for hours and even days, in which a person can feel hopeless and, at other times, excited.

REPTILIAN BRAIN: Colloquial name for the basal ganglia that sit in our forebrain cellar and contain the neural networks for activating our neurotransmitters. This area also relates to our daily rituals and routines.

SACRAL CORE OR PLEXUS: Sacral, meaning personal and holy, is located in our pelvic floor area beneath the base of our spine. The ancient mystics called this the seat of wisdom because of its powerful capacity to activate our physical and psychic energy patterns.

SPAZZING: A process in which the emotional, limbic brain vibrates in an intense purging and tension releasing activity. When expressed to a person it manifests as a vituperative outburst.

TEMPORAL LOBES: An area of the brain just above the ears where hearing and memory are located.

THALAMUS: The brain relay station that receives signals from all brain centers.

THYMOS: A command center located in the heart and chest areas where one experiences an energy center of joy, excitement, pain and sorrow.

YELLOW JUICE: Serotonin relates to mood regulation and sleep patterns.

YUP/YUPPING: Intellectualizing or abstracting a situation through cogitating and engaging frontal lobe mechanisms to define or describe what is transpiring at a spontaneous primary process/ communication level. A person who mainly relates to the world in this manner is described as living in Yupville.

D R. JOHN TWOMEY is a graduate of Boston University and a board-certified clinical psychologist, (ABPP). He is a fellow of the American Academy of Clinical Psychology and the recipient of the Distinguished Service Award from the American Board of Professional Psychology. He is an assistant clinical professor of psychiatry at Tufts University School of Medicine and on the senior faculty in the School of Psychology and Counseling at Cambridge College.

Dr. Twomey was a psychologist for four decades at the Veterans Outpatient Clinic in Boston. Throughout his career his passion has been focused on sharing with medical and mental health students his expertise on recovering from trauma and healing broken hearts. The focus of this therapy is to activate the patient's restorative healing energy patterns so that a meaningful quality of life and satisfying emotional relationships can emerge.

He is an avid baseball fan and was a youth baseball coach for many years. He and his wife live in suburban Boston and have four grown children and five grandchildren.

Made in the USA
Middletown, DE
21 November 2017